Praise for Reframing a Relevant Faith

Dr. Smith's text is both a wonderful introduction and a well-thought out defense of Progressive Christianity. He offers a way to reclaim God, the Bible, Jesus and the Church with intellectual integrity, relevance to our contemporary society and a challenge for us to return to the very inspiration for Christianity at its inception. For those interested in exploring Progressive Christianity, this is an ideal first source. He does warn that "too many Christians do not want to put the intellectual effort into thinking about faith … this book is my contribution toward calling Christians to think seriously and critically about their faith" (p. 13). He writes with passion, insight and intelligence, explaining his arguments clearly for any educated layperson and offering ample references for those who want to do their own digging. It could readily be used by lay-led study groups in the local church. His final chapter, on reclaiming the Church, urges us to return to the message, the methods, the motivation and the meaning that the historical Jesus originally imparted to his earliest disciples. It is a good and compelling read and one I heartily recommend.

David Moffett-Moore, DMin, PhD
Pastor, Portage United Church of Christ, Michigan
President of the Academy of Parish Clergy
Author of *Creation in Contemporary Experience, Wind and Whirlwind,* and *Life as Pilgrimage*

While America is awash in religion, Christianity has been in crisis. The popularity of reactionary fundamentalism is diminishing as it becomes another passing fad. It is amazing, however, that those leaving ecclesiastical structures and anti-intellectual, anti-scientific Christian ideologies are not attracted by the new atheists. They are still seeking meaning for their lives in the Christian gospel. These pilgrims will find in *Reframing a Relevant Faith* a worthy guide.

Herold Weiss, PhD
Professor Emeritus of Religious Studies,
Saint Mary's College, Notre Dame
Author of *Finding My Way in Christianity: Recollections of a Journey, Creation in Scripture,* and *Meditations on According to John*

Drew Smith has given us a clear and insightful presentation of progressive Christianity. Smith invites us not only to live the questions, but also to live in the style of Jesus. This text is profound without being preachy, and inspires the reader to claim a faith that is adventurous and world-changing. One of the best presentations of the progressive Christian vision I have read.

Bruce Epperly, PhD
Author of *Process Theology: Embracing Adventure with God* and *A Center in the Cyclone: Twenty-first Century Clergy Self-care*

Progressive Christian C. Drew Smith asks, "Is Christianity a religion that legitimizes intolerance, subjugation, and violence, or is it a faith of tolerance, equality, and peace?" Jesus, Smith explains, believed that God was presently acting in the world to bring about something new, a radical shift in the Judaism of his day. Joining the Jesus movement meant opposing the powers that carried out oppression, violence, and injustice, whatever those powers may be. Following Jesus is liberating, but it is also demanding. It is costly. If your Jesus permits you to wage unjust violence against your enemies in the name of national security, if he allows you to hoard money and possessions in the name of financial security, if he consents to your prejudices against people of other races, genders, religions and sexual orientations, then he is not the Jesus of the Bible. Smith's research, presented with humility and relevance, introduces us to the real gospel of the real Jesus. It's an unforgettable journey.

Lee Harmon, *The Dubious Disciple*
Author of *The River of Life: Where Liberal and Conservative Christianity Meet*

Reframing a Relevant Faith

C. Drew Smith

Energion Publications
Gonzalez, FL
2014

Copyright © 2014, C. Drew Smith

Scripture quotations are from the New Revised Standard Version Bible, copyright © 1989 National Council of the Churches of Christ in the United States of America. Used by permission. All rights reserved.

ISBN10: 1-63199-121-3
ISBN13: 978-1-63199-121-9
Library of Congress Control Number: 2014957827

Energion Publications
P. O. Box 841
Gonzalez, FL 32560

energionpubs.com
pubs@energion.com
850-525-391

Table of Contents

1. A Progressive Faith 1
2. Reclaiming the Bible 17
3. Reclaiming Jesus 49
4. Reclaiming the Church's Mission 81

 A Progressive Faith

He who rejects change is the architect of decay. The only human institution which rejects progress is the cemetery.
~Harold Wilson, Former British Prime Minister

The 21st century world is one that is in constant flux. The advances in technology, the continuing spread of globalization, and the growing interaction between diverse cultures presents our modern world with continuous and unstoppable change. This is indeed not the world our parents experienced, and it is most likely not the world we envisioned in our formative years. But this world has come to us, or rather has been created by us, and thus we can either try to stop such rapid change or we can invest our energy into reframing our lives to fit within this change.

While such flux does have an impact on every part of our lives, both individually and as a society, one important aspect of our lives that is feeling the weight of significant cultural, technological, and global shifts is religion and the values which are derivatives of religion. This is not to say that shifts in religious culture are isolated from other cultural changes, for any significant social, economic, and political shifts in a society will often result in a shift in that society's religious understanding and practice. For example, the Protestant Reformation, though often treated as primarily caused by religious forces, was as much a reaction to the political and social changes already occurring in Renaissance Europe. It is a fact that religious changes played a key role in the overall shift in Europe at the time, but only as a consequence of the social, economic, and political changes that happened as a result of the crises of late Medieval Europe and the rebirth of Renaissance Europe.

Eventually these changes led to the formation of differing Christian traditions, although Western Civilization remained solidly Christian. Yet, as these differing traditions formed, many searched for religious freedom, and they found such freedom in the new American experiment; an experiment that has flourished because of the freedom it has offered to all. Inherent in the idea of freedom, however, and particularly religious freedom, are the inevitable changes that have come to this nation over its brief history.

No one can deny that Christianity remains the most popular religion in America, although we must be clear that the United States was not founded as a Christian nation. While many who refuse to accept the changes we are experiencing would argue that the founding fathers did indeed establish our country as a Christian nation, the separation of church and state was clearly affirmed by the founders of this nation. Indeed, those who argue that America was founded as a Christian nation probably take this position due to the religious and cultural shifts they would like to see come to an end. Yet, even though it is inaccurate to say that America was established as a Christian nation, no one can deny that the Christian faith, in all its many forms, remains the most popular religion of all those practiced in the U.S. But in the sea of change in which we are currently trying to swim, the various forms of Christianity have either responded in reactionary ways against change or they have embraced such change. Much of this has not happened overnight, however, but has been developing for some time.

In the past history of American Christianity, people of faith mostly identified themselves with a particular brand or denomination of Christianity. One might be a Roman Catholic, a Presbyterian, a United Methodist, a Southern Baptist, or another of the many Christian sects that developed over the history of this country. These were identities people found comforting because they brought shape, context, and meaning to people's faith and lives. However, with the rise of the non-denominational movement in the second half of the twentieth century, these denominational loyalties slowly began to wane. Instead of finding a sense of connectedness to their parents' Christian denomination, people began to approach church with a consumer mentality, and traditional churches began to struggle to be relevant. In doing so, these churches sought to attract middle class folks to their congregations by offering a theology that looked more like self-help classes. These churches also made church a one-stop shopping institution in which people could find meaning and significance for every part of their lives. Moreover, as children of the 60s and 70s, many of these Christians were looking more for spirituality that they felt the traditional structure of churches and the traditional forms of worship could not give them.

Even established Christian denominations have experienced change on a grand scale, as each has had to wrestle, and sometimes battle, over both theological and social issues. Splits in denominations, like the Southern Baptists, have occurred along theological grounds as members fought over issues like the inerrancy of the Bible or the ordination of women to the ministry. More recently, the Episcopal Church in America and the Presbyterian Church U.S.A. have been debating the issue of homosexuality and especially how the church should respond to ministers in their denomination who are gay. And they are not alone in dealing with this issue on a large scale. These debates have created hostility and have caused folks on both sides to seek power and control of their denomination.

Moreover, significant social issues, like abortion and gay rights have become wedge issues across Christianity and have created unlikely associations. The late Jerry Falwell's Moral Majority and Pat Robertson's Christian Coalition put issues like abortion and gay marriage in front of these denominations and asked churches and their denominations to take a side. In doing so, they, and others like them, drew a line in the sand for some denominations, and people who once were part of the same faith began to move away from one another. Fellowship between believers was fractured not only by theological disagreements, but also by divergent views on social issues.

Good and faithful Christians began to stand on either side of these issues and this has produced unlikely coalitions between members of different Christian families. Some Roman Catholics,

Southern Baptists, and Conservative Presbyterians, as well as folks from other Christian denominations, are now siding together on these very issues, and they are looking across the fence at their one-time denominational brothers and sisters, with whom they once shared a common religious ancestry. While many still identify with their Christian heritage, they may be quick to point out that they are not like those from the same heritage who hold very different views on crucial theological and social issues.

Added to this phenomenon is a shift in the way religious folks voted in the 2008 presidential election. In past elections, at least since the election of Ronald Reagan as president, the Republican Party and its candidates have courted and held onto the religious vote. This was perhaps never truer than when George W. Bush ran for election in 2000, and then reelection in 2004. He, more than any other serious presidential contender, unashamedly courted the conservative Christian vote, and he was quite successful in garnering their support. At the same time, however, Democrats mistakenly avoided speaking about religion in the context of politics, preferring to treat religion as a private matter, and thus they conceded the importance of religion to people to the Republicans.

However, when running for president in 2008, candidate Barack Obama openly spoke often about religion, the value religion plays in a society, and his own personal faith. Though there were continuing, but unfounded rumors about Obama's own religion, whether he was a Muslim, and there were heated debates over the views and rhetoric of his then pastor, the Reverend Jeremiah Wright, Obama gave a religious voice to the Democrats that they had not had in generations. In doing so, Barack Obama was able to bring religious dialogue into the public and political arena without the stigma of the religious right. Moreover, he reframed some of the social issues in such a way that faithful Christians on both sides of the debates began to think about common and middle ground on these issues, instead of moving to the extreme poles on either end of the political spectrum. In doing so, he won many religious voters who had been otherwise committed to the conservative agenda on those social issues they felt were of upmost importance, and we witnessed a rising of the religious left.

What these changes tell us is that there is a growing grassroots Christianity that has become more open and more progressive in its understanding of belief and practice.[1] Many Christians have become weary of the theological and political battles, seeing them as distracting the church from its authentic mission in the world. Moreover, many of these Christians are beginning to understand the importance of working with others, regardless of religious affiliation or no religious affiliation, for the common good of the world. And, while many still remain faithful in confessing the historic creeds and beliefs of Christianity, they are also embracing the idea that Christianity is more about practice than about what one believes. All of this has and will continue to have an effect on the way Christians live in a society undergoing constant change.

The Great Emergence

Author Phyllis Tickle has called what Christianity is currently experiencing "The Great Emergence," and she likens the current shift to the Protestant Reformation of the sixteenth century.[2] While time will be the only judge of whether we are experiencing something akin to the Protestant Reformation, the Christian faith, and the church that embodies that faith, is certainly going through noteworthy challenges and adjustments.

Tickle succinctly articulates her understanding of the forces that have begun to shape what has become known by many as the emerging church. While this movement is yet to be clearly defined,

---

1   We should also note the selection of the first Latin American Pope as a sign that the Roman Catholic Church is experiencing radical change. Pope Francis, the name Jorge Mario Bergoglio took when he was elected Pope, is being viewed by many in the Catholic Church as a reformer and one who is very concerned with the teachings of Jesus, particularly as they related to the oppressed and poor. Indeed, it appears that the Vatican may no longer disapprove of Liberation Theology (http://vaticaninsider.lastampa.it/en/the-vatican/detail/articolo/teologia-della-liberazione-freedom-theology-teologia-de-la-libertad-vaticano-vatican-25842/).

2   Phyllis Tickle, *The Great Emergence*.

and this may be part of its mystique, it is growing in popularity among those who come from both strong denominational ties as well as those who have no church background whatsoever. Tickle uses the image of a rummage sale as her overarching metaphor to describe what happens to the church every so often. By her estimation, about every 500 years the church needs to clean house and it seems that it is currently due for a cleaning; since we are a half-millennium away from the Protestant Reformation, which Tickle views as the last church rummage sale.

My intention is not to deal specifically with Phyllis Tickle's book, or with the phenomena of the emerging church, but perhaps we are experiencing something akin to the Protestant Reformation. Perhaps, given the monumental social and cultural shifts we have witnessed in the last few decades, especially since the beginning of this new millennium, Christianity is in the middle of a rummage sale, to use Tickle's metaphor. If so, we need to reframe how we understand Christian belief and practice, particularly those central tenets of the faith.

Yet, while I appreciate the labels "emerging" and "emergent Christianity" to describe what is happening in many corners of the church today, I prefer the term progressive. This may only be a semantic difference, but it is, at least in my mind, an important distinction. I certainly did not coin this particular term, for it has been in use for some time and in various pockets of Christianity.[1] But to me the term progressive seems to capture more of what I think and believe about the growing faith movement.

For me, the term progressive Christianity suggests a faith that is moving forward; a faith that is progressing toward what God desires from and for humanity. Yet, at the same time, progressive Christians do not negate the value of the past, and especially the sacred text and traditions of that past. Progressive Christians take the Bible seriously, but not always literally, and they are open to thinking critically about the BIble. As a progressive Christian, I am interested in doing the serious work of biblical interpretation that

---

1 One good web-based source on the progressive Christian movement can be found at The Center for Progressive Christianity at www.tcpc.org.

values the Bible as a sacred text, but that also understands these texts as having a very complex human origin.

Progressive Christianity is not about intellectually accepting a set of propositions about God, Jesus, and the Bible. Rather, being a progressive Christian is about being transformed by Jesus' teachings and way of life. It is about finding one's existence as a follower of Jesus in this life. It is about living one's life here and now.

Moreover, the idea of being a progressive Christian implies one who is open to new and different ways of knowing and experiencing God. Instead of simply declaring that this or that religious idea is truth, as a progressive, I am more interested in the conversations about what truth is and how we find it. I am more interested in the journey on the path that will lead to truth than in saying I have found that truth.

Thus, as a progressive Christian, I cannot assume that the way I think about God or the way my religion tells me to think about God is definitive. Human knowledge about the divine and the language we use to describe the divine are limited, and any revelation a religion may claim to have about God is also limited. No sacred text is any more valid than the other in the claims it makes about God, for all of them, including the sacred text of Christianity, are human ways of expressing how a particular tradition understands God.

But perhaps the greatest reason I am a progressive Christian is that I find at the heart of Jesus' teachings not a message of forensic salvation from one's sins, but rather a message of transformation that leads me to deny myself, take up my cross and follow him in self-giving service to others. In this sense, progressive Christianity is certainly about spiritual transformation, the transformation of the self. But it is also about social transformation; transforming our societies in ways that reflect the central ideas of Jesus: love, compassion, inclusion, justice, and peace.

Thus, from my perspective, the progressive Christian movement looks different than what we have experienced before. Regardless if one accepts this movement as valid or not, one must admit that it is a product of the cultural and religious shifts we are seeing across the span of Christianity. In other words, Christianity itself is changing, whether we like it or not, and we are entering, or have already entered, a post-Christian world, and even perhaps a post-Christian America.[1] Thus, those of us who choose to remain Christian, but at the same time seek to make our faith relevant in this changing world, may find hope in this progressive movement. Given this fact, this book is my contribution to the ongoing conversations about the relevancy of Christian faith in this post-Christian world.

The Necessity of a Critical and Relevant Faith

If a relevant and progressive Christianity is to survive and bear witness of God's love to the world, the adherents to such a faith, those who seek to follow Jesus, must embrace a critical approach to the Christian faith. Critically thinking about the faith is not equivalent to criticizing the faith, as some may think, although that may be part of critical thinking. Rather, thinking critically about the faith is to continue to ask questions, to inquire about the history of the faith, its present relevancy, and its future hopes. It is also to admit its flaws and weaknesses with honesty and transparency.

For this to happen with any degree of success, any question about the Bible, theology, and the practice of faith must be taken as a valid question. In dealing with the mysteries of God, we should never be completely satisfied with the idea that if the Bible says it, then that settles it. Nor should any of us be entrenched in our own interpretations of scripture. We should always be open to new ways of thinking about the Bible and theology, for to do so leads us toward the truth and the realization that, in the words of Jesus, the truth will set us free.

I have no doubt that many readers of this book will quickly identify with what I have to say. At the same time, I have no doubt that just as many others will find what I have written to be difficult to accept, and they may even reject these ideas outright. I am not

---

1   A report by the Pew Research Center indicates a rise in those who do not identify with a specific religious tradtions, the "nones." Morevoer, this study reports that 37% of those surveyed call themselves "spiritual" but not religious. http://www.pewforum.org/2012/10/09/nones-on-the-rise/.

so bold as to think I have figured it all out. However, I would like to offer my own story that has led me to many of the ideas I am arguing in this book.

Readers of this book will find out rather quickly that I am a person who seeks always to ask serious questions about faith. I don't ask these questions to be provocative, and I am not simply playing the "Devil's Advocate." I am also not seeking to create a straw man that I can easily attack. I am asking such questions with a great deal of honesty about my own interpretation of the Christian faith that has evolved over many years. There are specific reasons why I asked such critical questions, and why I encourage others to ask challenging questions.

One reason for my determination to raise critical questions about faith, and why I encourage others to do so, is that I grew up in a fundamentalist tradition in which queries about the Bible and faith were not appreciated. This was particularly true when one tried to ask questions about the inconsistencies found in the Bible, or when one tried desperately to harmonize a belief in a good God with the reality of suffering. As a teenager, I was told that such questions are not important, and even heretical to ask; only knowing Jesus and believing in him were necessary. I was satisfied with this answer until a later time when I began to discover the intellectual obstacles one encounters when approaching the Bible for definitive answers. It was then that I returned to ask those serious questions, which opened more questions, and which eventually led to evolutionary, and indeed revolutionary changes in the way I view the Bible and the Christian faith. I can say with all honesty that this shift in my thinking did not come easy and it took time. In fact, I fought this for some time until I realized that venturing into unchartered waters, at least uncharted for me, led me to a deeper and more satisfying faith.

A second motive for my critical look at the Bible and Christian faith is that I have perceived an insufficient education in our faith and in the Bible on which our faith is based, particularly in churches. By this I don't mean that churches are doing a poor job at doing Christian education. Many churches are doing a fantastic job at providing training in the faith to their members. But there may be a bit of shallowness to the education we provide, in the sense that we are not always struggling with tough questions. There is no doubt that asking tough questions may lead us down paths that we dare not want to travel, but such questioning may be necessary if we are to make our faith our own.

This deficiency in the kind of Christian education that promotes critical thinking has led not only to biblical illiteracy, but more tragically, to ignorance when it comes to biblical interpretation and theological thinking. Many Bible study groups do not seriously consider the complexities inherent in reading ancient texts. Rather they focus only on what these texts say to us as individuals, as if the books of the Bible were written with our needs in mind. Furthermore, churches are not providing tools to help folks think theologically. Instead, theology becomes a separate box of propositions we always believe, without critically assessing their value for our context.

Of course, much of the fault lies with those who print such materials for church groups. Some materials produced for the purpose of Christian education are often so insipid and limitedly focused that they only serve to heighten our emotional experiences without moving us into a deeper and more thoughtful understanding of God and humanity. While finding personal meaning from the Bible and from our faith is vitally important for Christians, it is secondary to and flows from delving deeply into the text of the Bible to discover something outside ourselves and our own narcissistic needs. The popular idea that God wrote the Bible for me needs to be stamped out.

Failure to do so will only lead us to assume what the Bible says, or will cause us to make the Bible say what we want it to say without giving careful thought and attention to the text itself. Moreover, such Bible readings will limit our understanding of our faith to simply a personal spiritual experience.

Reframing a Relevant Faith

The title of this book, *Reframing a Relevant Faith*, was developed with great intention. As intelligent humans who are constantly receiving messages and signals through various mediums and experiences, we process these messages through our own frames of reference. These frames of reference are formed by our own histories, our own cultures, and our own beliefs, whether religious or not. In terms of religious beliefs, many people use religion as the primary way to understand life. Theology is always formulated in context, whether the theology that is shaped is formal or personal. While the Bible and our Christian traditions have significant influence on shaping our theology, our experience will eventually play a major part in what we develop as our theology. This may happen on a personal level when one experiences something good or something tragic that alters his or her understanding of God and life. But it can also take place on a wider scale.

The theology that has been passed down from generation to generation, whether based on the Bible or tradition, or some combination of both, becomes ours, but only after we have re-framed it to our own world and our own experiences. This means that we must take seriously the texts of the Bible, the creeds and confessions of the church, and the historic theology and liturgy of our Christian heritage. But it also means that we need not transfer all of this to our own context as if the Bible, the creeds and confessions, and the historic theology and liturgy of our Christian heritage were stone tablets. We have to re-frame these in order that theology becomes relevant for every context.

This may not be an easy process, and it is certainly not a willy-nilly method. Moreover, we may hold out as long as we can before we embrace such change and re-frame our understanding. Indeed, those who are fundamentalists are called this for the very reason that they do not accept these changes to their fundamental understandings about the Christian faith, and thus they will refuse to re-frame religious beliefs, choosing instead to hold on to what they see as revealed and unchangeable truth. Yet, even those who identify themselves as liberal have their own traditional beliefs that will be difficult for them to reframe.

But those who do embrace this change, whether joyfully or reluctantly, must somehow re-frame their understandings of their beliefs about God, the Bible, and the Christian faith to fit their own context. Re-framing can mean minor adjustments to what we believe about our faith, or it can be major paradigm shifts in the way we think and believe. This is not a haphazard or insincere approach to theology and faith, for we must remain in dialogue with the scriptures and the traditions that have been passed on to us. In re-framing our faith, we may not completely throw out the old in order to make room for the new.

Why This Book?

This book is my attempt to re-frame how we think about the central ideas of Christian faith and practice as a result of the cultural and religious changes of our modern world. In a sense, what is contained in this book, at least to some extent, is how I understand progressive Christianity. My proposals in part or in total are not exhaustive interpretations of progressive Christianity; they are merely my contributions to what I perceive as a growing conversation about the meaning of progressive Christianity and the future vitality of this movement.

As I stated above, if the church is to do more than survive the current and inevitable changes that are occurring and to remain relevant in the midst of these shifts, then we must re-think and re-frame Christian belief and practice. Therefore, in the chapters that follow, I will discuss how we might rethink the Bible, Jesus, and the life and mission of the Church. By stating that we should rethink these Christian tenets, I am not suggesting that any of these are outdated, or that any of these important theological ideas should be thrown out. Indeed, what we believe about these is vitally important to Christian identity; without any of these we cease to be Christian. Nor, am I suggesting that my ideas will be accepted by all. I am not so bold as to claim to have definitive ideas on these topics. My reason, indeed, my hope, for writing this book is to contribute to the ongoing conversation about Christian faith as it is shaped by the beliefs and practices of changing Christians living in a changing world. I also hope to engage believers from all persuasions in this ongoing conversation.

While I am trained in biblical scholarship, I have not written this book primarily for scholarly consumption. Theology and theological thinking are not owned by the academy. I do believe that many Christians have mistakenly rejected the work of very fine academic scholars and theologians, believing that somehow because they work in the academic world, they are focused on deconstructing the Christian faith to make it seem untrue or illegitimate. Simply rejecting ideas about the Bible and theology just because they are formulated in an academic setting seems ill-informed at best. Indeed, our reading of the Bible and our understanding of church history and theology will be much better informed if we pay attention to what scholars and theologians are saying.

But most theology and theological thinking takes place within churches at the grass roots level, and scholars who dismiss this reality are only fooling themselves. Thus, I seek to be in dialogue with both sides of the conversations, but especially those taking place at the grassroots level. Yet, as one who holds a Ph.D. in New Testament, and one who has been trained in history, biblical studies, philosophy, and theology, I also seek to provoke a deeper theological thinking from these churches. Too many Christians do not want to put the intellectual effort into thinking about faith, and this is a problem that must be remedied. I hope that this book is my small contribution toward calling Christians to think seriously and critically about their faith.

I have written this book not only as a book to be read by individuals, but also one that I hope will be used in groups. Indeed, reading this book in community may bring great dialogue about the issues raised here. Theological thinking and faithful discipleship does not happen when individuals uncritically consume information. Rather, good theological thinking happens in conversations between persons who think different and who come together from different back grounds to pursue questions. Thinking, discussing, and debating issues and ideas in community leads to more faithful churches that seek to follow Christ in authentic discipleship.

My hope is that this book causes folks to think critically about their faith. Therefore, to this end, I have provided questions at the end of each chapter that I hope will spur on critical thinking and good conversations. Moreover, I hope that these questions will lead to both individuals and groups creating more questions. The pursuit of truth is always an endless pursuit, and this often requires new ways of thinking. Or, as St. John of the Cross stated, "To come to the knowledge you have not, you must go by a way in which you know not."[1]

To take this journey we must continue to ask probing and sometimes uncomfortable questions. Such questions, perhaps uncomfortable, and maybe even frightening to ask, can help to lead us down the never-ending path of pursuing the truth. May we continually ask such questions about our faith, individually and together, in an effort to reframe a relevant faith.

---

1 John of the Cross, *The Ascent to Joy.* Marc Foley, ed. (New City Press, 2002), p.68.

Questions for Reflection and Discussion

1. How do the changes we experience in society shape how we understand our faith?

2. How do personal changes influence how our faith changes and develops?

3. What effect has your background had on your religious thought?

4. Why is it important to continue to ask critical, and sometimes uncomfortable, questions about our faith?

 # RECLAIMING THE BIBLE

Another century and there will not be a Bible on earth!
~Voltaire

Voltaire (1694-1778), the French Enlightenment philosopher, who is quoted above, was wrong in his prediction of the Bible's demise, for not only does the Bible have a long and rich history in Western society, it remains the world's best selling book. Its wisdom has brought many people comfort in times of sorrow, distress, and confusion and its stories have spoken to the hearts of believers for generations. Yet, the reality is that many folks who read the Bible with great sincerity and faith may not be familiar with the many critical issues surrounding its origin, the differences in one Bible from another, the complexities of interpreting the Bible, and the problems inherent in trying to make the biblical material relevant to our modern world. More tragically, historical evidence demonstrates that the Bible has also been used as a tool of power, oppression, and violence against individuals and people groups.

In this chapter, I hope to lay out some critical and foundational issues about the Bible that can inform us to be better readers and interpreters of this sacred text. Why begin with the Bible and not God or even Jesus? After all, is not theology about God and is not Christian theology specifically about God's revelation in Jesus? The answer to both of these questions is yes. But any discussion of Christian theology must start with the texts of the scripture, for Christian understanding, though not limited to using the Bible as its only source, must surely begin there. Thus, an honest and thoughtful understanding of the Bible is necessary to develop further theological thought and discussion.

While some may avoid these issues that are discussed in this chapter and take the Bible at face value, and still others may completely avoid the Bible as a source of faith and dismiss its importance altogether, I prefer to face the questions head on and to formulate a more critical understanding of the Bible that can inform our faith. In my view, a serious and robust faith is not based on intellectual apathy, but grows from asking the most difficult and troubling of questions. This does not mean that we cannot glean something very meaningful from simply reading the Bible. Indeed, this is the nature of literature; to move the reader to experience something via the story or poem through the simple act of reading. But if the Bible is to serve as a source of Christian faith and practice, then we must dig deeper into the Bible and its history, which compels us to ask some very critical questions. A good place to begin is to start with the question of the Bible's origin and how it came to us.

The Origin and Transmission of the Bible

If we are to come to some understanding of the Bible as a source of faith and practice, then we must also become aware of the Bible's origination and development. Though some would like to believe that the Bible fell from heaven, in King James English, wrapped in nicely bound leather, with the words of Jesus in red, most people know that this is simply not the case. The history behind the writing, copying, and compiling of the books of the Bible is much more complicated, but certainly much more interesting.

Many well meaning Christians believe the Bible consists of the very words of God. By this, they either imply or state outright that each word of the Bible was inspired by God through human scribes who simply recorded every word that God spoke to them, a theory known as verbal inspiration. While such a view still seems very prevalent in many churches, this opinion does not take seriously the historical setting of the Bible, or the history of the Bible itself. If we are to read these texts faithfully, then we should come to understand them as historically situated texts written by historically situated human authors who had their own views of God, humanity, and the world.

This is not to suggest that the Bible is not relevant to the needs and cares of our world; needs and cares of both a collective people and as individuals who seek to know God. I will address the relevancy of scripture for our modern living later, but for now we should seriously consider that accepting the historically situated nature of the various books of the Bible is the only way we can explain the many diverse views we find throughout the Bible. Humans who wrote these books did so from their own perspectives of the world and how they thought God was working in the world. Moreover, they had their own assumptions about the world, and the texts they produced contain those assumptions that make it very difficult for them to offer timeless truths that apply to our lives in a more complex and interconnected modern world.

Indeed, the authors of the biblical texts were so limited to their own space and time, as are we, that their claims about God do not fit other claims about God from other biblical authors. We can even see that some parts of the Bible come into conflict with other texts in the same canon. The most significant of these is the strange difference we find between the God of the Hebrew Bible, who is portrayed as authorizing war and violence, and the God of the New Testament that is described by the person of Jesus as the God of peace. Of course, God is not always portrayed as a warrior God in the Hebrew Bible , and Jesus himself makes statements that seem to suggest violence as legitimate (Luke 22:36), but we still must admit that various understandings of God exist even among the different authors of scripture.

Honestly admitting this reality raises the issue of whether or not the Bible is inerrant. I have chosen not to see the scriptures as inerrant, for the word inerrancy calls for so many qualifications that the term loses any real meaning. For example, the Chicago Statement on Inerrancy adopted in 1978, and the standard-bearer of inerrancy for most conservatives, states that the scriptures are inerrant and infallible in the autographs, that is the original manuscripts penned by their original authors.

Yet, these original manuscripts no longer exist, and any knowledgeable scholar of the Bible can tell us that the variety of copies of biblical texts that we now posses demonstrate errors, whether they were intentional or unintentional.[1] It is true that through the discipline of textual criticism scholars can establish closely what we believe to be the original readings of these texts, and it is also true that scholars can offer reasonable explanations as to what changes to texts occurred in the copying process, but this does not negate the extant evidence of texts with errors. While most of these errors, known as variants, are minor, and rarely do they present serious challenges to the most important doctrines of Christianity, there are some among the New Testament manuscripts that are quite significant.

For example, while most English Bibles continue to include Mark 16:9-20 at the end of Mark's Gospel, a reader of this passage should see a note in her English Bible that informs her that this ending does not appear in some of the most reliable ancient manuscripts. In fact, the curious reader of the end of Mark is offered three optional endings, one called the longer ending, which includes Mark 16:9-20, one called the shorter ending, which essentially contains a paragraph that follows Mark 16:8, and the one most scholars believe to be the original ending, which ends at Mark 16:8. Yet, there have been a handful of scholars who have suggested that there was an ending to Mark past 16:8, but it has been lost.

While the majority of scholars prefer the ending at 16:8 to be what was original to the Gospel of Mark, there are some who argue that the longer ending of Mark could very well be original to the writing of the Gospel. In fact, in the Pentecostal tradition, this text stands as a fundamental narrative, and perhaps one of the most important passages of scripture in the entire Bible. Thus, there is a theologically invested interest in demonstrating that Mark

---

[1] Scholars refer to the discipline of seeking to discover the original reading of a text from multiple and diverse copies of that text as Textual Criticism. For a readable analysis of textual problems see Bart Ehrman, *Misquoting Jesus* (HarperOne, 2005). For a more thorough, but much more technical book, see the classic text by Bruce Metzger, *The Text of the New Testament* (Oxford University Press, 1992).

16:9-20 is original to the narrative.[1] Still others have a theologically vested interest in proving that this ending is not original and that the Gospel ends at 16:8.

We also find that many important manuscripts do not contain the famous story about the woman caught in adultery in John 7:53-8:11. This story is so touching and meaningful to most folks that when I have pointed out to them that the story is most likely not original to John's Gospel, they have reacted with great consternation and even outrage at my questioning the very words of God. But, as I explain to them, saying that the text is not original to John is not the same thing as saying the story is not historical. This does not mean the story did not happen, but it does mean that the passage was most likely not in the original text of John. But raising this question must cause us to rethink our understanding of the Bible, and most importantly the history of its transmission.

There are other important variant readings across the scope of the Bible that we could discuss, but the mention of these two is enough to raise serious questions about what many have called the inerrancy of the Bible. Moreover, these variations in readings also demonstrate that the Bible has a history that has been influenced by humans from its origins, through its transmission, down to its translation. When turning to consider the canonization of the Bible, that is, how the collection of certain books became the sacred text of scripture, we must also consider seriously the historical, and therefore, human process of the formation of the Bible in its final form. I can only deal here with the formation of the New Testament, and how this became the canon of the Christian Bible.

The word "canon" comes from the Latin word that describes a reed that was used to measure. The term took on the meaning of standard or rule. Thus when we speak of the "canon of scripture," we are speaking about the books that were recognized as the standard, the rule, or the measure of authority for faith. The canon is what is recognized as sacred text.

---

1 See for example, John Christopher Thomas and Kimberly Ervin Alexander, 'AND THE SIGNS ARE FOLLOWING': MARK 16.9-20—A JOURNEY INTO PENTECOSTAL HERMENEUTICS, *JPT* 11.2 (2003) 147-170

It was inevitable that Christianity would become a religion with a sacred text. Inheriting a collection of texts from their parent religion, Judaism, early believers in Jesus not only read Israel's ancient books differently than their fellow Jews who did not believe Jesus to be the Messiah, they also began to develop their own set of texts, some of which would eventually become the New Testament. This was an historical process that involved human decisions that would define the Christian Bible. It was an historical decision-making process that would result in some books being included in the canon, while other books would be left out.

Over the period of time between the life of Jesus and what we should cautiously refer to as the "closing" of the New Testament canon, texts were written, copied, and passed from church to church. Because of the flux intrinsic to such an historical process, we cannot say with any degree of certainty that what would eventually become known as the New Testament was acknowledged by these early Christians. Indeed, there is no evidence that a New Testament in the exact shape we know it today existed for centuries.

What was the historical process that led to twenty-seven books becoming the New Testament? Logically, step one of this progression was the writing of texts in response to what early followers of Jesus believed about him. In their experience of Jesus, they believed they were experiencing something new from God; a new revelation that would lead them to formulate stories to tell to others, first in oral tradition and then in written form.

But the impetus to write was also caused by the needs of Christian communities that developed after the death of Jesus. Scholars have long known that the epistles we find in the New Testament were written to address problems in certain Christian churches. One only has to read Paul's letters to the Christians in Corinth to see that the Apostle was writing to answer questions and address problems that existed among these Christians. The same is true for other New Testament epistles. But scholars have also argued that the Gospels show signs of addressing community situations.

For example, many scholars have argued that the Gospel of Mark was written to a community that was perhaps facing persecution, and that the community to which Matthew is written was probably very Jewish. Thus, the writing of these texts was not primarily for historical reasons, but out of the necessity to address community needs.

This being true, the subsequent step in the process of these texts becoming canon was the reading of texts in worship. If Paul's letters, written earlier than the Gospels, were written to address problems in the churches to which he was writing, then we can logically argue that his letters were being read in these congregations. Moreover, the Gospels, with Mark being the first one to be written in the late 60's to early 70's, give evidence that they were addressed to particular Christian communities, which would mean that they were read in these churches. Indeed, in Mark 13:14, the author offers direction to the one who publicly reads to the congregation, "Let the reader understand." While we can pick up a Bible at the local bookstore, or even better, access the text via the Internet or a smart phone app, the ancient world relied heavily on the oratorical reading of texts. We might add that such public reading from one voice was in itself a practice in interpretation, for the voice's inflection and stress on certain words or phrases could alter meaning in the hearing of the audience. Yet, the important thing to remember here is that the public reading of these texts in the context of worship would have caused them to be viewed as authoritative scripture, growing out of the Jewish practice of reading scripture publicly.

Moreover, viewing these texts as scripture to be read in worship would lead not only to the copying of these texts, but also to their dispersal to various Christian communities. Churches would swap texts with other churches, as is suggested by the writer of Colossians who commands, "And when this letter has been read among you, have it read also in the church of the Laodiceans; and see that you read also the letter from Laodicea" (Col. 4:15). Of course, we don't have the letter to the Laodiceans that is mentioned by the author of Colossians, but the command to read the letter suggests a public reading.

What would the effect of public reading and sharing of texts have on the status of these written documents? Perhaps much like many Christians do today, certain texts would become more meaningful for certain groups of people. In other words, certain books would perhaps be more important than other books, much like Christians today have favorite verses or favorite books. As such, it is conceivable that the public reading and the sharing of writings with other churches led to some books becoming authoritative for some churches, while other books would not be viewed as scripture by these churches. Some Christian communities may favor some texts, while other Christian communities would favor different texts.

We must also consider that in this process, other texts would come on the scene and become important for certain Christian communities. As Christianity spread away from Jerusalem, Christian texts would become more diverse. Other Gospels would be written that would be important to various Christian communities. This diversity may have been so widespread that it would have been impossible for wide-ranging agreement on the Christian canon to take place across the vastness of the Roman Empire.

Indeed, books such as Hebrews and 2 Peter, which were not necessarily viewed as scripture by many churches, would become part of the New Testament. Other writings, such as 1 and 2 Clement and the Shepherd of Hermes, were viewed as scripture by many churches, and yet they would not be included in the books of the Christian Bible. Therefore, we do not have overwhelming evidence that a universal New Testament existed before the fourth century. Rather, various Christian communities may have held their own canons as authoritative. But for many church authorities, this kind of pluralism would not do, and they sought to bolster what they determined as orthodox.

While there were always those on the fringe of this orthodoxy, the popularity of the teachings of a man named Marcion (85-160 C.E.) presented a significant threat to the church authorities. Marcion excluded the Hebrew Bible or Old Testament and included in his scriptures only ten letters of Paul and a particular version of Luke, free of any references to Jesus' Jewish heritage.

Marcion's influence was significant enough to gather a large following as well as the attention of church authorities. The popularity of his teachings, even long after his death, as well as the beliefs of other communities deemed unorthodox, convinced church leaders that a defined canon of scripture needed to be finalized. This would be the only way to root out potential challenges to what church authorities considered to be the developing orthodoxy.

But it was not until 367 C.E. that a list of the twenty-seven books was affirmed as the canon of the New Testament. This canonical list appears in a letter written by a bishop named Athanasius and excludes those books considered heretical by the church, as well as some books that were popular even among orthodox Christians. By the time of this letter, the Council at Nicaea (325 C.E.) had already defined in specific terms what orthodoxy was, and thus teachings outside of their definition would be regarded as heretical. Thus, what appears to be the final step in closing the canon of scripture was a move brought on by Constantine's gift of power to the church. The church authorities, now backed by Constantine, determined that what went into the sacred text was orthodox.

This historical process demonstrates that as Christianity developed some Christian groups, in response to what they believed about God and in reaction to opposing views from other Christian groups, made decisions about what would be called the New Testament. Looking back on this process raises certain questions about the range of the canon of scripture, about who determines what the Bible is and says, and to what extent the scriptures serve as the sole basis of authority for Christian faith and living.

The Canon(s) of Christian Scripture

We must be careful, however, when we speak about what we refer to as the canon of scripture. While most of you who are reading this book are probably Protestants who have lived all of your lives knowing one Bible that includes thirty-nine books we call the Old Testament and twenty-seven books we refer to as the New Testament, we should realize that other traditions recognize different books that are as much authoritative to them as the books others recognize as scripture. Various traditions within the Christian faith differ in the books accepted as holy writ. Indeed, throughout the history of the church, the canon of scripture has been debated and has never really been conclusively settled except within each specific tradition.

Space prevents an extensive discussion of the differences between canons across the time and space spectra of Christianity, as one could write a whole, and indeed, lengthy, book on the topic. But to raise the significance of the question over the canon of scripture, I will mostly concentrate on the variations between the Roman Catholic and Protestant Bibles. However, we should be aware that churches in the Eastern Church also differ in what they view as canonical.

For example, early in its history, the Syrian Church accepted as scripture a writing known as the *Diatessaron*, an amalgamation of Matthew, Mark, Luke, and John into one. They also accepted fourteen letters associated with Paul, including a third letter to the Corinthians as part of their canon. Later, this tradition would accept the four Gospels, along with the Pauline corpus, but they rejected II Peter, II and III John, Jude, and Revelation. The Ethiopian Church, which has existed since the early centuries of Christianity, recognizes forty-six books as the books of the Old Testament and thirty-five writings as their New Testament, which includes the twenty-seven traditional books as well as eight additional writings not found in other Christian canons.

These examples may be insignificant to many of us, for many Western Christians are unaware that these other Christian traditions even exist. But these examples should raise questions concerning who determines the scope of the Christian canon. Yet, even in the history of the Western Church, there exist significant differences between two canons of scripture; one affirmed by Roman Catholics and the other by Protestants.

The Roman Catholic Old Testament follows what is known as the Alexandrian Canon, which is associated with the Septuagint, an ancient Greek version of the Hebrew Bible. This canon consists not only of books accepted by Protestants, called *protocanonical* by Roman Catholics, but also additional books known by Roman Catholics as *deuterocanonical*. Protestants do not accept these additional books as canonical and refer to them as *apocryphal*.

The Roman Church affirmed its canon long before the birth of Protestantism, and has reaffirmed it at the Council of Trent in 1546, and in more recent history at Vatican Councils I (1870) and II (1960s). Yet, Protestants deny this canon and only recognize the shorter number of books. What brought about the difference between the canons of these two Christian traditions?

The *deuterocanonical* books came under serious scrutiny and were rejected as scripture by leaders of the Protestant Reformation of the 16th century. This was due in part to the popularity, brought on by the Renaissance, of reading ancient texts in their original languages. Protestant Reformers, who were greatly influenced by the Renaissance, sought to read the Old Testament in Hebrew, thus favoring the Palestinian Canon. The Palestinian Canon is the name given to the Old Testament that is written in Hebrew and which contains a shorter number of books.

But the most significant reasons for excluding these *deuterocanonical* or *apocryphal* books were theological. Most Reformers attacked central theological teachings of the Roman Church, such as purgatory, and so they dismissed certain books as teaching such false doctrines. From the position of attacking these doctrines, they then determined that these books were not divinely inspired, and thus should not be considered scripture. Again, it seems reasonably clear that theological positions led to what books would be included in the canon and which ones would be left out.

However, although some Protestant leaders refused to see these books as canonical, they did include the *deuterocanonical* or *apocryphal* books in their translations, designating them as useful for devotional reading. Even the Authorized Version of 1611, better known as the King James Version, included these books and placed them between the Old and New Testaments.

In 1647, however, the Westminster Confession of Faith declared these books as non-canonical in the Protestant Church stating that they, "not being of divine inspiration, are not a part of the Scripture." Eventually these books would be omitted from Bibles published by Protestant Bible Societies, forever sealing the fate of these books in the Protestant tradition.

It should also be mentioned that some Reformers, most notably Martin Luther, also questioned some of the New Testament books. Luther doubted the canonicity of Hebrews, James, Jude, and Revelation, placing these four at the back of his 1522 German New Testament, stating in the preface to Hebrews, "Up to this point we have had to do with the true and certain chief books of the New Testament. The four which follow have from ancient times had a different reputation." Erasmus, upon whom Luther relied for his Greek text, also doubted the authority of these four as canon. But Luther was particularly troubled by the Epistle of James. He found James to be "an epistle of straw with no character of the Gospel in it," for James clearly states that a person is justified by works, thus challenging Luther's doctrine of salvation, which emphasized *sola fide*, salvation by faith alone, apart from works. Thus, even after eleven and a half centuries, the makeup of New Testament was still being disputed.

Word of God and Words of Humans: Rethinking Divine Inspiration

It should be clear by this point that though there is largely agreement as to what constitutes the canon of scripture, there are significant differences in the way Christian traditions define the canon. While each tradition holds firmly to their belief that their respective canon is the authoritative word of God, a critical question becomes ever more important when we consider the historical processes and the decisions that were made, as well as the various results that these decisions produced. What does this mean for understanding the Bible as inspired? Christians have long believed that the Bible was inspired by God, basing this doctrine on Second Timothy 3:16, which states, "All scripture is inspired by God." The word translated as "inspired" literally means "God-breathed," and although the author of these words would have been speaking specifically about the Hebrew Scriptures, Christians would most certainly include the books of the New Testament as those inspired by God. But what do we mean by "inspiration"?

Most seminary students can list the various theories that have been proposed to describe the action of divine inspiration. From those theories that view the scriptures as produced by gifted human authors, to the idea that God gave a message to the author, who then used his own words in writing the text, to the theory that God dictated every particular word of the text, each hypothesis has been debated by theologians across the range of Christian thought. Indeed, schisms in denominations and local churches have happened over disagreements over how one defines inspiration. Moreover, professors of theology have been fired from their institutions and excommunicated from academic societies based their definition and explanation of divine inspiration.

While 2 Timothy 3:16 clearly states that "All scripture is God-breathed," this does not mean that we must accept the idea that every word was dictated by God to the human author, who then recorded those words. Again, if we take the author of 2 Timothy seriously, we can only admit that this verse is in reference to the Old Testament or Hebrew Bible. Yet, even if we recognize the New Testament as inspired by God, it is not compulsory to believe that every single word of the text was inspired by God. One's critical approach to scripture or to any theory of divine inspiration does not in and of itself negate one's faith in God or the Bible as a source of faith. To view the text of scripture as having a human origin as much as a divine one does not make one less faithful in one's belief in God, and is really more intellectually honest with the evidence.

In fact, the texts of scripture actually give more evidence to human involvement in their production than they do of divine inspiration. This does not mean that we need to throw out divine inspiration altogether. But we must ask two very important and interrelated questions if we are to define, at least at some level, the idea of inspiration. Why did the writers of the books of the Bible write and why did they write what they wrote?

Those holding to verbal or literal inspiration would answer that God led these biblical authors to write what they wrote. This may be true at some level, but there is no way for us to know this. In fact, a critical and historical investigation of the Bible, as I have suggested above, leads us more in the direction of concluding that these authors chose of their own free will to write and to write what they wrote. Thus, it might be helpful for us to answer the questions about why these texts were written, and why the authors wrote what they wrote, by considering why the two communities that produced the two portions of the Bible would have done so. In approaching the question from this angle, we are being more intellectually honest with the text.

Obviously, we must speak here in generalities when we talk about ancient Israel, from whom we received the Hebrew Bible, and early Christianity, from whence comes the New Testament. Across the time and space of both of these communities, but particularly ancient Israel, there was much diversity that has become a part of the text of scripture.

The people of Israel viewed themselves as different from the other nations that surrounded them. They believed their God was supreme over other gods, and that their God had created the physical world from nothing and had chosen them as a covenant people. This belief certainly influenced their understanding of the world and other peoples, but it also influenced the telling of their stories, both orally and then through written texts.

To put it succinctly, Israel's texts of scripture came forth from the people of Israel in response to what they believed about God and what God was doing. In other words, they were theologically interpreting history and they were telling their history from a theological point of view. Their understanding of God and the world influenced the way they told their stories, from the creation story, to the flood story, to the Exodus story, to the stories of conquering the land of Canaan through violence, and the stories of their Exile and their return.

In approaching an understanding of the writing of the New Testament books, we must remember two things. First, the earliest followers of Jesus were Jewish, and hence any faith that would develop from their experiences must have some connection to ancient Israel and its texts. Second, because these earliest followers of Jesus believed him to be the promised Messiah of Israel, they must be able to explain this in relation to God's working in the life of ancient Israel as expressed in the Hebrew Scriptures. To state it differently, early followers of Jesus needed to make their texts point to Jesus as the promised Messiah and they needed to tell the stories of Jesus in ways that harmonized him to their texts.

In holding onto these two important ideas, the authors of the books that would become the New Testament searched the Hebrew Bible in an attempt to understand and explain Jesus. While we like to think that the Old Testament foretold the coming of Jesus, it is probably better to say that those earliest believers in Jesus saw in him what they believed was described about the Messiah in the Hebrew Bible. In other words, in their experience of Jesus, they re-read their ancients sacred texts, looking for texts that made sense to their understanding of Jesus, and then applied those to Jesus. They then formulated their stories about Jesus to define his life, teachings, death and resurrection as the fulfillment of God's ancient promises. Thus, their experience of Jesus influenced both their reading of the Old Testament as well as their writing of the New Testament.

Yet, what also influenced the writers of the New Testament was the current situation of the churches to which they wrote. As stated above, the documents of the New Testament for the most part were shaped as much by the needs of the communities of faith as they were by the stories that were passed down about Jesus. Certainly we are aware that Paul's letters, as well as the other epistles, were written to churches that were dealing with issues. But we must also be aware that embedded in the Gospels and other New Testament books are the situations of the followers of Jesus during the time of the writing.

What all of this means is that the text of scripture, what we call the Bible, is the Word of God in the sense that it contains the stories of how God's ancient peoples believed God to be working in the world. For these two communities of faith, the writing of these texts was the formation of a theological explanation for the existence of the world and humanity, a theological diagnosis of the human predicament, and a theological explanation for overcoming this predicament. The Bible contains the explanations of the mysteries of God envisioned by these historically situated humans, but no more. Their understanding of God, humanity, and the world is much different than our own. Though we can learn from them and are influenced by their stories and texts, we must approach these texts critically in order to assess how the Spirit speaks through scripture today.

The Bible and the Gospel Truth: A Four Gospel Test Case

So far, I have attempted to lay out briefly the historical issues surrounding the origination and canonization of the Christian Bible. Evidence suggests that human involvement and decision making was the important component to bringing what we call the Bible into the form we know today. This does not dismiss God or God's inspiration, but the evidence we have points more toward human involvement than divine inspiration. But if this is the case, does this understanding of the Bible challenge the truthfulness of the Bible?

I have been asked on a number of occasions whether I believe the Bible to be true. I have always answered the question, "Yes." Those who have pressed me further on this issue generally require me to say that everything in the Bible really happened just as it says. It is then that the conversations usually come to an end, for I usually tell my inquisitor that for something to be true does not mean that it really had to happen in the way that it is told.

From a faith perspective, the Bible is true in the sense that it reveals what its authors experienced and believed to be true about God, humanity, and the world. It is also true in terms of its message of hope and salvation that has been received and experienced by people throughout time and space. And it is true because it continues to be a collection of living texts that shape the lives of those who consider it as a source for their understanding of God. But is the Bible entirely factual, as in historically accurate? The answer to that question is more complicated.

For most of Christian history, questions were seldom asked about the historical reliability of the Bible. During the period in which the books of the Bible were written, copied and eventually collected, and during the Medieval Period, in which religious truth was considered to be the ultimate truth, the historicity of the Bible was never under question. However, with the coming of the Renaissance, when Christian humanists began to be concerned with the texts of the Bible in the original languages, and then when the Scientific Revolution opened serious questions about what the Bible says about the universe, there followed the period of the Enlightenment in which critical challenges to the historical reliability of the Bible were being made. Such questions were especially concerned with discrepancies in the four Gospels of the New Testament.

Are there discrepancies in the Gospels? The answer is yes, and here are just a few that relate to important events in the life of Jesus. In reporting the baptism of Jesus, both Mark and Luke state that the voice from heaven declares, "You are my beloved son," indicating that Jesus is the only recipient of this revelation. Matthew records that the voice says, "This is my beloved son," implying that more than Jesus hears the voice. Although parts of the baptism narrative are mentioned in John, the Fourth Gospel does not actually narrate the baptism of Jesus, a very peculiar omission. When we consider how each narrative treats Jesus' cleansing of the temple, we find that in Matthew, Mark, and Luke, Jesus does this at the end of his ministry. In John he does this at the beginning; the timing of which is historically unlikely.

Moreover, while all four Gospels tell of the death of Jesus, they vary somewhat in the details about the crucifixion. John even narrates that Jesus dies on a different day than he does in the other three stories. Finally, in the empty tomb scene, while two messengers appear in Luke and John, one messenger appears in both Matthew and Mark. However, in John these messengers appear after Peter has come to the tomb and not before. And although the resurrected Jesus appears in Matthew, Luke, and John, he never does in Mark, if we take Mark as ending in 16:8, which as I stated above, is what most scholars of Mark believe. What are we to make of these inconsistencies as a challenge to the truthfulness of the Gospels?

First, we must recognize that the Gospels, like other stories in the Bible, were not written primarily to record history as are historical accounts written in the modern world. The Gospels were composed for the primary purpose of telling the story of Jesus from a theological point of view in order to encourage faithful discipleship in those who chose to follow Jesus. Though they tell a history, and they serve us as a source of historical evidence to understand who Jesus was, they were not written for the purpose of proving historical information as modern biographies are, and if we are honest, we must admit that some of what is found in these narratives may not have really happened, or at least not in the way that the gospels tell them.

Second, the Gospels are crafted theological interpretations of Jesus' life. Jesus was a real historical figure, who lived as a first century Jew, and who died on a Roman cross. These facts are historically accurate.[1] Moreover, many of the acts and teachings of Jesus that we find in the Gospels are historical as they can be traced back to the historical Jesus. Yet, in their encounter with him, Jesus' closest followers experienced him in a much different way than did others, and this experience shaped the way they told his story. Although most of their stories are based on historical events in the life of Jesus, the Gospels that take shape beginning in the late 60s to early 70s with Mark, are interpretative theological representations of a real historical figure, even if the facts are not always as accurate as our modern minds would like them to be.

While we historically and factually minded modern people may be troubled by what some see as inconsistencies between the

---

1 There are some who argue that Jesus did not really exist at all. These "mythicists," as they are known, have very little credibility when it comes to historical research. Even the not so conservative agonistic scholar of early Christianity, Bart Ehrman, points out their flawed argument in his *Did Jesus Exist?: The Historical Argument for Jesus of Nazareth* (HarperOne, 2013).

Gospels, we need not dismiss their value for informing and forming our faith. Whereas we look to the Gospels for historical information about Jesus and the early Christian movement, more than anything, we read them from a faith perspective, meeting Jesus through the stories, and finding our place in his story. In this encounter with Jesus, we are not so much asked to believe all of the so called facts about Jesus, as we are called to follow him in faithful discipleship. It is this way of reading and living the Gospels that expresses the real truth of their stories.

The Bible and Science

For over a century debates have raged over the ability of the Bible to tell us about the world, particularly how the natural world, and beings that inhabit this world, came into existence. These debates have only continued the supposed animosity between science and the Bible that started with the 17th century Scientific Revolution when Galileo challenged a literal reading of the words of scripture by showing that the sun, and not the earth, is at the center of the universe, and that the universe functions because of mathematical laws. Yet, in our politically charged culture, the conflict between the Bible and science seems more heated than ever.

The issue is fundamentally about whether the Bible can answer the questions of science. Or, to put it more bluntly, which tells us the truth, the Bible or science? Of course, at the heart of the current conflict is the contentious debate between the scientific theory of evolution and the religious belief in creation. The challenge of science to faith has become so threatening that attempts have been made by some who hold to a literal reading of Genesis 1-2 to use a form of pseudo-science to propose a theory known as intelligent design; but at its core, this teaching is only a refurbishing of creationism. The problem with this view lies in our misunderstanding of the first chapters of Genesis as a basis to prove the idea that the natural world was literally created in seven days from nothing.

Admittedly, I am not a scientist, so I cannot speak about scientific theories in much depth, and certainly not in this brief portion of a book chapter. But, as I see the problem in this tense relationship, I am not convinced that it lies with those on the side of science. This is not to suggest that science is always right, or that science can answer all our questions about the world and human existence. Indeed, science cannot fully answer these questions, and if we think it can, we have merely moved to the opposite end of the spectrum and replaced religion with scientism. However, as one trained in biblical scholarship and theology, I can address what I see to be the problem from an interpretive and theological point of view.

First and foremost, we must understand that the narratives of Genesis were written by ancient humans, who, without the skill of modern science, sought to explain their world and the origins of the natural world from a religious viewpoint. Genesis, then, was the ancient Hebrews' story of their beginnings and the origins of the world and humanity as they saw it from their theological, but not scientific, point of view. Like other ancient peoples, the Hebrews justified their religion and their view of the world by telling their creation story, which detailed how the world came about as an act of their God.

In the case of the Hebrews, the Genesis narrative was an attempt to define their God as the supreme God of the universe, who is transcendent, and who, in God's infinite wisdom and power, created the physical world, including humanity, represented by the characters of Adam and Eve. Thus, the beginning chapters of Genesis are *theological* narratives that express how the Hebrews viewed their God as supreme over other gods, a theme that continues throughout the Hebrew Bible. But the Genesis narratives are not scientific accounts or explanations about natural phenomena, and they cannot support such a literal reading.

We must remember that these historically situated ancients sought to explain the world, just like we seek to explain the world, but they did not have available to them the history of scientific discovery or the technology of scientific advancement. Instead, they crafted a narrative of creation, focused not so much on how things happened, but why they happened. The creation story is about God's relationship to humanity and human relationships with other humans and creation itself, but we need not read it as a literal explanation of how the earth and the humans who live on this earth came about. Stressing a literal reading as that which is the only acceptable one misses the point of the narrative.

Does this view dispel any notion of God? The answer to this question is simply no. While some who hold to evolution as the answer to the origins of the natural world do dismiss the idea of a divine being, science cannot prove or disprove the existence of God. Alternatively, neither can the Bible prove that God exists. The Bible can only describe how ancient people of faith, Jews and Christians, understood God. A belief in God comes only through faith.

Is evolution a threat to the authority of the Bible? The answer is again no. The Bible is theological literature, written by ancient people, who wrote from the perspective of their religious faith and how they understood the world, humanity, and the divine. The creation story from Genesis is a theological explanation of the world from a monotheistic Hebraic perspective, but it is not a scientific explanation.

Thus we must approach the Bible not as a scientific document, for the scriptures cannot answer our scientific questions. Rather, we must view the Bible as a religious text that shapes the way we should live out the image of our God in our world through our relationship to God, to other human beings, and to creation itself.

The Bible and the Illegitimacy of Divine Violence and Oppression

One of the fundamental reasons that many want the Genesis narrative to be an accurate account of creation is so that we can view creation not so much as a gift from God to be cared for and cherished, but as a means to an end. Those who hold this view tend to embrace the idea of being dominant over creation. More important, however, those who hold to the literal interpretation of the Old Testament do so as a means of rationalizing violence towards and oppression of certain segments of the human population.

For all of the good that religion does in our world through the generous acts of people from all faiths, much attention has been given over the last few years to evil acts performed in the name of religion. The relationship between religion and violence, oppression and subjugation is not new to the world, and no single religion monopolizes evil done from religious conviction, as Western Christians tend to think. Christian history demonstrates that the Christian religion has often been used as a pretext for supporting demeaning attitudes and violent acts against others.

At the pinnacle of the Medieval Church, Christians slaughtered Muslims, persecuted Jews, and tortured "heretics" all in the name of God. During World War II, one of Hitler's reasons for exterminating millions of Jews was that, in his mind, the Jewish people were responsible for Jesus' death. Since the birth of the modern State of Israel, conservative Christians have mostly supported Israel's oppression of Palestinians because of a misguided apocalyptic theology. Even in more recent days, Christian preachers continue to goad for an apocalyptic war between the Christian world and the Muslim world. And Christian faith is frequently a basis for intolerance of people because of gender, race, or sexual orientation.

Is Christianity a religion that legitimizes intolerance, subjugation, and violence, or is it a faith of tolerance, equality, and peace? More importantly, what does the Bible say about violence and oppression, and how do we solve the theological conundrum that views the Christian faith as a peaceful religion when parts of scripture sanction oppression and violence? To answer these questions, we need to consider why the Bible might seem to authorize intolerance and violence, and then we need to propose how to read the Bible from a critical position that recognizes that not every part of the canon exhibits normative patterns of behavior and values.

An exhaustive discussion of how the Bible legitimizes oppression and violence would take a more extensive investigation than I can offer here, but a good place to begin is with ancient Israel's war against the people of Canaan. While the Hebrew Bible tells the story of God ordering and giving Israel violent victory over their enemies, we need to consider that these stories were expressed from a backward looking theological interpretation.

This was not an uncommon way of viewing victories in the ancient world. In the ancient world, one's victory over one's enemies was always the victory of one's god over the gods of one's enemy. This means that when we read the stories of the Bible, we need to think critically about these narratives and question whether or not God actually gave authorization for this violent conquering of the land. If we do not, we run the risk of forming a theology that legitimizes religious intolerance, subjugation, and violence.

Yet, since these stories are included in what the church has affirmed as the Word of God, how do we handle a canon of scripture that at times sanctions demeaning attitudes and violent acts toward others, but at other times calls us to promote peace, love, and justice in our world?

First, we have to come to the conclusion that every text of the Bible must be understood within the norms of its original context, and thus the initial commands and behaviors offered in particular texts do not necessarily apply equally to the contemporary world. Indeed, forcing certain "principles to live by" from some of these texts will only lead to misguided theology.

A case in point is the way some biblical texts seem to place females in inferior positions to males. The society of the first century viewed women as inferior to men, and thus the biblical commands that limit the rights of women reflect the society at large, even if theological reasons are given for supporting male authority over women. This viewpoint has not gone completely away in our modern world.

One pertinent example is the prohibition against female pastors in the Southern Baptist Convention, as well as in other denominations. This represents a form of exclusion that denies one gender the right and privilege to serve a calling from God that is as equally valid as that issued to males. While those holding a position that forbids women from serving as pastors claim that their position considers women as equal in essence to men, they deny that females are equal in the role they play in the church, particularly in leadership positions. But such religious chauvinism has not stopped at banning women from the pulpit.

In recent years there has been a robust and calculated push to put women under the rule of their husbands. Instead of affirming the biblical egalitarian view that sees husbands and wives as equal and co-submissive to each other, this position claims that even in the modern world men should rule women and specifically in the confines of marriage. Tragically, a couple of years ago, one Southern Baptist theologian suggested in a sermon that some spousal abuse is the fault of women who do not submit to the rule of their husbands. His rationale is that when a husband's leadership is threatened by a wife who is not submissive, that husband may respond with abuse. He clearly places the blame on the woman. Gender inequality in the home and in the church, as well as other issues of inequality and repression, represent the idea that theology can be a powerful weapon of authoritarianism.

However, we cannot, and we must not, read the Bible in this way. Rather, we should recognize that as the rights of women have progressed in the modern world, the particular biblical texts that are used to support the subjugation of women, or any other population for that matter, should no longer be normative for how we see folks who have been historically marginalized from full participation in the work of the church. Instead, we should deconstruct these texts in light of Jesus who preached a gospel of equality and justice.

Second, we must understand that not every part of the Bible witnesses equally to God's character and will. The Bible was not written by God, but was written by historically situated humans who were seeking to understand God, humanity, and the world. Thus, those passages of scripture that picture God as one who legitimizes demeaning attitudes and violence must be assessed in light of those that speak more fully about the God who loves all human life. A faithful reading of the Bible must give careful attention to the original meaning of a biblical passage, but such readings must also give preference to those texts that testify most clearly to the God who is discovered in the teachings of Jesus. Thus, for Christians, the words and deeds of Christ serve as the interpretative filter through which we must understand all scripture.

From a Christian point of view, Jesus' authority has primacy over other portions of the Christian Bible. Scripture's normative message of God's desire to love and redeem all humanity calls us to repent of our intolerance and violence toward others, and opens our hearts and minds to authentically love our friends and enemies through acts of peace and generosity, not oppression and violence.

Is the Bible the Only Source of Theological Authority?

The progression of this chapter from a brief analysis of the historical questions about the origination and formulation of the Bible to historical, scientific, and ethical problems associated with reading the text today has brought us to a crucial question. Can scripture stand on its own as a basis of authority? On the one hand, we would have to answer this in the affirmative. The stories of scripture, both from ancient Israel and early Christianity have stood the test of time and, although they have been translated and transmitted down through history, they have stood on their own authority and have influenced the faith of millions across time and space.

On the other hand, given the fact that these texts have been translated, as well as interpreted since their beginning, we would have to at least qualify our affirmative answer to the question of whether scripture alone is the authoritative basis of Christian faith and practice. That is to say, a text, though standing on its own, can only have meaning through the exchange between text and reader. Meaning may be found in a text, but meaning does not come to life until the text is read and interpreted.

One of the foundational theological shifts that occurred during the Protestant Reformation was an emphasis on the sole authority of scripture as that which is sufficient for faith. Indeed, while Martin Luther is known for challenging the Roman Church most notably on the issues of indulgences and salvation by faith alone, his arguments were based on his belief that theological doctrines must be based on scripture alone, or *sola scriptura*, and not on any church authority, whether bishop or council. This belief continues to serve as one of the hallmarks of Protestant Christianity, particularly in free church traditions.

Yet, even so, it is difficult to say that *sola scriptura* has ever been fully practiced even in Protestantism. Indeed, Protestant confessions that have developed since the time of Luther and his fellow reformers are in and of themselves interpretations of scripture. Moreover, the commentaries that began to appear from the Protestant leaders, most notably Luther and Calvin, lay out a Protestant faith that is an interpretation of scripture. Thus, even these great heroes of the Protestant faith do not allow scripture to stand on its own, but offer their own interpretations of scripture.

Yet, in the 18th century, a new leader in the Protestant tradition, John Wesley, the founder of Methodism, re-framed the understanding of the authority of scripture in what has become known as the Wesleyan Quadrilateral.[1] Many historians, however, believe that the Wesleyan Quadrilateral was most likely developed by Albert Outler, a twentieth century Methodist theologian, who derived this way of viewing scripture from John Wesley's writings. From whatever source this methodology developed, we can use it as a way of recognizing the authority of scripture, but not as the sole authority.

In the quadrilateral, scripture holds primacy of place for normative Christian understanding and practice, but there exists an interdependent relationship between scripture, church tradition, personal experience, and logical reason. Scripture serves as the foundational authority for the church through its time and space existence in the world, but scripture must be interpreted in light of church tradition, personal experience, and logical reasoning. In this sense, scripture is what the human biblical author believes to be the revelation of God to his specific historical situation, the time of the text, but that revelation lives on the existence of the text and the interpretation of the text in future generations who must rely

---

1   For more on the Wesleyan Quadrilateral see Michael Kinnamon and Jan G. Linn, *Disciples: Reclaiming Our Identity, Reforming Our Practice*, Chalice Press, 2009; and Don Thorsen, *The Wesleyan Quadrilateral: Scripture, Tradition, Reason, & Experience as a Model of Evangelical Theology*, Emeth Press, 2005.

on tradition, experience, and reasoning to formulate meaning for the church in its current context.

This means that although the text of scripture still serves as a basis of authority for the church's faith and practice, indeed it must remain as such, each generation and locality of the church must find its own interpretations that are in conversation with the text of scripture and church tradition, but that are open to the influence of personal experience and logical reasoning. In this way, the Bible still remains valid as a source of Christian faith and practice, but the literal understanding and interpretation of the Bible now has a more rational filter through which the text can be sifted so that it remains relevant.

Thus, *sola scriptura*, or scripture as the sole authority of faith and practice, is a misnomer, and does not reflect the reality of how the text of scripture has been used and continues to be used in the church. Indeed, it is erroneous to suggest that sola scriptura has ever really been practiced. While the reading of scripture in worship and community is important, someone must interpret the text in order to formulate legitimate interpretations that represent the fullness of the gospel of grace and peace in each and every context.

Critical and Communal Interpretation of the Bible

Regardless of which Christian tradition we call our own, the sacred texts of the Bible are always central to that tradition. While we may affirm different canons of scripture, all families within the Christian faith have great reverence for the scriptures and view them as having a vital place of authority in shaping Christian belief and practice. Yet, we must realize that the texts of scripture never stand on their own. The Bible does not interpret itself, but must be interpreted by those who read the text; those situated in various times and places who seek to grasp what these texts say about God.

There are many reasons people may read the Bible, e.g., historical or literary, but the ultimate and constant reason for reading the Bible is theological. Most who read the text, or hear the text read, believe it to have something to say about God and God's engagement with humanity. Indeed, the Bible exists, both in its parts and in its whole, not primarily for historical or literary purposes, but because both the parts and the whole of the Bible offer the historically situated authors' views on God and how God relates to humanity. In other words, the authors of the different books of the Bible present primarily a theological perspective of life from their own world.

But the very existence of the Christian sacred texts from any and every tradition indicates that the stories of the Bible are not just about the events, characters, and times of their own era. These stories extend beyond their own frame of reference to communicate a belief in God's good future in which each generation can find hope in the midst of the challenges of human existence.

So, if the primary purpose for writing the books of the Bible and for reading these books is theological, then how should we read these ancient texts that were written by historically situated humans who would not have envisioned the world in which we live? Do we take what they say about God at face value, or should we be open to fresh understandings of God? Answering these questions fully would take more space than allotted here, but I want to offer at least a rudimentary approach to reading the scriptures theologically.

One important step to reading the Bible theologically is to embrace a critical approach to biblical interpretation. In other words, we can extend our critical approach to the Bible past simply asking questions about the history of the Bible, to asking questions about what the Bible says. A critical approach to reading scripture is not only appropriate, it is also necessary when one is seeking to develop relevant theological thinking.

A critical approach involves several components that contribute to viable and meaningful interpretations. Reading the Bible critically means not only giving close attention to the literary nature of the text, and to the genre of a specific text, but also to the historically conditioned nature of the biblical texts and the authors who penned them. These authors, and the texts they produced, reflect a different worldview than ours. They viewed the cosmos differently, history differently, and the experience of the divine differently. Thus, any faithful readings, and the theology that develops from those readings, must take into account the assumptions these authors had that we no longer have. While developing our theology from the scriptures must demonstrate integrity with the historical meaning of the text, our readings are not bound by those original meanings as we seek to bring theological relevancy to our own context.

Yet, as we read and interpret the text of scripture to this end, we must also recognize our own presuppositions. Each of us reads from our own ideologies that are often culturally transmitted to us.[1] We approach the biblical text with these ideologies, which often leads to our reading our presuppositions into the texts of scripture without realizing it. Our gender, our race, our sexual orientation, our socio-economic class, and even the various events we have experienced and continue to experience all contribute to the assumptions we have about what the Bible says and means. Moreover, we often do not recognize such ideologies and presuppositions, and not doing so can cause us to cling consciously or unconsciously to misunderstandings and misinterpretations of biblical passages that are not true to the text or a critical approach to its interpretation.

Indeed, such misinterpretations may be so deeply embedded in our cultural locations that they may be hard to set aside altogether. They are often like a pair of old spectacles that have become a part of who we are and through which we see everything. To be sure, we would be uncomfortable and untrusting of what we read without them. But, if we are to read the texts faithfully in order to shape a more relevant and meaningful theology and practice, we must take them off, at least for the purpose of seeing the text differently.

Of course, we could read the Bible critically in isolation, but that may only lead us back to our presuppositions. A more fruitful practice of reading would be to read the text of scripture in a community that may offer challenges to our individual understandings. A text of scripture does not have a single meaning limited to autho-

---

[1] See V. George Shillington, *Reading the Sacred Text: An Introduction to Biblical Studies* (London: T&T Clark, 2002), 5.

rial intent, and no one person has greater authority in interpreting a text of scripture. Certainly we can be helped by those trained to read these ancient texts; those committed to the study of their original languages, settings, and purpose, but we need not all be biblical scholars to read, appreciate, and live out the meanings of the biblical texts.

Each of us approaches the texts with different experiences and thus each of us has different presuppositions. When shared in a community of textual readers, however, such experiences can enrich one's faith and lead one to be more faithful in his or her discipleship. The richness of the biblical texts cannot be limited to authorial intent or authoritative interpretation. Rather, the Bible contains a multiplicity of valid interpretations, and reading in community can help us see other meanings and other ways of assessing the Bible.

Yet, while we can read the scriptures in the communities we call our churches, this may only reinforce the same presuppositions. Others from our community wear similar glasses, for we typically associate with those who look like us, talk like us, and are from the same social and economic situations. There is nothing inherently wrong with this practice, and reading in like minded community is an exercise in biblical and theological interpretation that can shape our discipleship. But, reading the text with people from other races, other cultures, other social and economic conditions, and other ways of thinking about God and humanity can help us recognize our presuppositions and assist us in seeing the text vastly different. And such a practice may help us to see God differently by offering the Spirit a way of leading us to fresh interpretations that shape our theological thinking.

Why the Bible is still relevant for Christian faith

While it may seem that my thoughts in this chapter reveal that I am not one who believes the Bible has any real purpose for our faith, this is not the case. The Bible must remain the primary source for our faith and practice as followers of Jesus. Indeed, it is only through these texts of scripture that we come to know the

Jesus of history, who calls us to follow him in salvation and discipleship. The Bible is thus the living story that speaks to our hearts and minds about how we ought to live as faithful disciples of the one we call Savior and Lord.

But such a view of the Bible does not diminish the need for us to critically approach and appropriate the Bible to our modern contexts. The Bible has a long and rich history that gives it significance and meaning, but it also makes it necessary to read and understand its meaning through critical and reasonable understandings that are relevant for our faith today. While we may not take the Bible literally, we must take it seriously, especially as we seek to allow the text to shape our faith and practice in the world. Doing so not only gives us hope in its ancient words, but it also moves us closer to our ultimate demonstration of the truth of scripture; following Jesus in authentic discipleship.

Questions for Reflection and Discussion

1. What do the historical issues surrounding the Bible, i.e. its development, its historical situation, and its canonization mean for people who read the Bible to find theological truth and encouragement for faithful discipleship?

2. Why is it important to understand how other traditions view the Bible? Does respecting and even validating these other traditions compromise your own?

3. What does it mean to say that the Bible is inspired by God?

4. How can we read the texts of scripture both critically and from a faith perspective?

5. How do we balance the Bible as a source of faith and practice with our current experiences?

6. How can reading the Bible in community with others who are both like us and very different from us help shape our theology in conversation?

 Reclaiming Jesus

For Christians, the unending conversation about Jesus is the most important conversation there is.
                                                    ~Marcus Borg[1]

Marcus Borg, one of the foremost authorities on the historical Jesus, is correct. From its inception, Christianity has been christocentric, that is, the life, teachings, death and resurrection of Jesus are central to the Christian faith. Indeed, there is nothing more central to Christianity than how we understand Jesus. This does not mean that Christians have always had a homogeneous view of Jesus, but in all the various forms of Christianity that have developed since the first century, Jesus has always been the central figure.

Yet, Jesus remains a somewhat enigmatic figure, whose life has been written about by thousands of authors, scholars, and lay persons alike. Moreover, Jesus' teachings still speak to our modern world and how we live in that world. This means that each Christian generation must not only reaffirm the centrality of Jesus to the faith, and therefore seek to rediscover Jesus, each must also seek to understand and implement Jesus' life and teachings in each and every context; a task that is often treated as easy, but when attempted with any seriousness, is very difficult.

Who was this Jesus? What do the Gospels tell us about Jesus? Does Jesus' life and words have meaning for us, and if so, how do we appropriate them for our own living as his followers in the contemporary world? These are the questions we must address if Jesus is to remain the central figure of Christian faith.

---

1 *Jesus: Uncovering the Life, Teachings, and Relevance of a Religious Revolutionary* (HarperCollins, 2006), 311.

The Historical Jesus and the Jesus of the Gospels

One of the most hotly debated topics among biblical scholars, theologians, and historians is the quest for the historical Jesus. Since the time the four Gospels came under scrutiny after the Enlightenment, scholars have taken a skeptical approach to reading these early stories of Jesus. From Hermann Samuel Reimarus, the 18th century philosopher, to David Friedrich Strauss, the 19th century German theologian, and then to the well known Albert Schweitzer, whose book, *The Quest of the Historical Jesus*, published in 1901, set the standard for Jesus research, modern scholarship followed suit, reading the Gospels with a critical, and even skeptical eye, doubting much of what the authors reported in these narratives.

While the study of the historical Jesus has been enhanced by the discovery of the Nag Hammadi scrolls, found in Egypt in 1945, these scrolls, and what they tell us about other views of Jesus, have added more difficulty to discovering exactly who he was, what he said, and what he meant by what he said. Moreover, all of this has contributed to significant challenges to traditional views about Jesus, his life and teachings, and most importantly, the interpretations of his death.

In more recent years, the Jesus Seminar has garnered significant attention from both scholarly and popular audiences as those scholars who are a part of the Seminar challenge the historical accuracy of the Gospel narratives, using colored beads to vote on the authenticity of Jesus' words and deeds. Such practices have given rise to responses from scholars who hold more traditional views of Jesus, and also to more nuanced interpretations of Jesus. One may not agree with the methods and conclusions of the members of the Jesus Seminar, but one should appreciate the honest questioning these scholars bring in their attempt to find the Jesus of history as well as the new focus they have brought to Jesus study.

Using various literary, historical, and sociological methods, scholars have re-framed and re-framed the issue over the historical Jesus attempting to ask questions not only of the historical accuracy of the Gospels, but also of the events that influenced Jesus' life and mission, how he really viewed his life, his mission, and his relationship to Israel's God, and what theological interpretations of his life, mission, death and resurrection cloud our view of the historical Jesus.

The essays and books on this subject abound, as do the various theories proposed by scholars across the field. I cannot deal fully and properly with these in this book, and it is dangerous to push them all aside with a stroke of the key board, but my primary focus is upon the narratives about Jesus, for it is these stories that inform us most about him.

In fact, to manage the vast amount of information about Jesus that we find in the four canonical Gospels, I will concentrate mostly on what we find in the Gospel of Mark. I concentrate on Mark because it is the first Gospel to be written, sometime in the late 60's or early 70's of the Common Era, and Mark's Gospel formed the core that influenced the other two Synoptic Gospels, Matthew and Luke. Mark is a major source for Matthew and Luke, both of which expand the material we find in Mark. Thus, my primary focus will be on Mark, but I will also rely on the other Gospels at certain points in offering my understanding of Jesus.

Understanding Jesus through Mark does not negate the historical Jesus, for one must take a historical approach to the narrative in order to understand the historical setting of the Gospel, particularly in the religious and political environment of the first century Roman Empire. But, Mark is primarily a work of literature, a story about Jesus, and thus the primary focus will be on Mark's literary presentation of Jesus.

Jesus and Israel's God

One significant point that must be made from the outset is that Jesus was a first century Jew. While most today know this to be true, an appreciation of the influence of Judaism on the life and mission of Jesus has only recently become important. Many Christians might agree that Jesus was Jewish, but they may see Jesus' Jewish faith and identity only as a precursor to his founding of the Christian faith. Indeed, in my years of teaching, I have often asked this question on an exam: "What religious faith was Jesus?" The majority of students answer that Jesus was Christian. But Jesus was thoroughly Jewish and remained so throughout his life. Jesus never was what we consider to be Christian.

Yet, when we say that Jesus was a Jew, we must be careful to point out that this does not assume that Judaism was homogeneous in the first century. Much like Judaism today, and Christianity for that matter, first century Judaism was eclectic. While scholars have recognized the importance of the four dominant sects within Second Temple Judaism, the Pharisees, the Sadducees, the Essenes, and the Zealots, the largest population within Judaism, and the one Jesus was from, was the common Jews, the *am haaretz*, the people of the land.

The Gospels clearly indicate that Jesus was not from one of the ruling groups of Judaism, the Pharisees or Sadducees. While it is possible that the Essenes, that sectarian community believed to be responsible for the Dead Sea Scrolls, had an influence on John the Baptist, who then influenced Jesus, there is no convincing evidence that Jesus was associated with the Essenes. And, it is highly unlikely that Jesus was a Zealot, for his teachings on peace and non-violence is not parallel to their ideas about revolution. Jesus was born into poverty and remained a member of the common class of Jews living in the volatile world of first century Palestine.

As a Jew, however, Jesus held in common with other Jews that the God of Israel, who had been revealed through creation and covenant, was the supreme God who had chosen Israel and had redeemed them out of Egypt. Jesus, like many of the Jews of his day, was looking for God's new redemption of Israel from the chains of their oppressors. He was looking for a New Exodus, not from the enemies in Egypt, but from the power of Rome. He accepted the traditions passed down through Israel's history that God had set Israel apart as God's people and had made a covenant with them to be their God. He also believed that Israel had lost her way, as all the prophets testified, and that Israel's current plight would only be ended by an act of God. So, at one level Jesus' consciousness of God was influenced by tradition.

Yet, we also must consider that Jesus' awareness of God was also greatly informed by his own experience of God. Indeed, though he, like many Jews of his day, believed God was going to redeem Israel from Roman oppression, he took on this vocation as his very own mission. While we can point to various events in the life of Jesus that shaped his experience and understanding of God, as well as his own understanding of himself, including his upbringing under the weight of poverty and injustice and his constant encounter with the suffering of his own people, the Gospels suggest that one specific event seems to have played a particular role as the call to mission for Jesus. In his own baptism, Jesus witnesses the opening of heaven and hears God's commission for him to live out his identity as God's chosen son, the one sent to bring judgment on God's enemies of unjust power and oppression, and restoration to God's people. This religious experience perhaps gave affirmation to Jesus as to who he needed to be and what he needed to do.

But, in his experience of God, Jesus became cognizant of a God that could not be defined by tradition. While he accepted the traditional Jewish views of God, monotheism, creation, and covenant, he also gained, in his own experience of God, an alternative to the tradition. So what did Jesus believe about God?

Foremost in Jesus' mind was the belief that God was presently acting in the world to bring about something new that would radically shift the Judaism of his day. Nothing clarifies this more than Jesus' announcement that the kingdom of God had come. Later is this chapter, we will turn attention to the concept of God's kingdom in the teachings of Jesus, but for now I think it very right to assume that Jesus believed that God was not simply the God of Israel's history who had somehow become distant. Rather, Jesus' God was now present in the world, overthrowing the powers of evil and establishing God's own rule.

Jesus believed that God was establishing a new order in the world, one that reversed the oppressive power of injustice and inaugurated a world of compassion, justice, and peace. In Jesus' mind, the world had become chaotic, oppressive, and filled with injustice. But he believed that God was presently restoring order and justice to the creation, and Jesus acted on this understanding of God. His miracles serve as vivid metaphors of God's power to release the captives and to overthrow the powers of the world, and his teachings proclaimed a new ethic that would continue to bring order and justice to creation. In this sense, Jesus lived out his vocation as the envoy of God's rule.

But Jesus also understood and communicated that God was not concerned with the formal religion that was practiced in Israel, apart from the ethical living demanded by God, particularly having love for one's neighbors and enemies. While he did not seek to abolish the Law, as he came to fulfill the Law, he did challenge the assumptions others had about the Law, that it was merely the outward pious actions of the religious. Instead, Jesus declared that God was concerned about the inner being of a person and the motivations of a person's heart that produced acts of goodness.

It seems clear from reading the Gospels that Jesus' most severe challenge was aimed at the formal religion of his day, and more particularly at the religious elite that controlled religion, when he cleared the temple. It may not have been the temple itself, or the sacrificial system within its walls that Jesus found troubling, although certainly it very well could have been. What seems certain, however, was that Jesus was angry at the abuses that resulted from a religion that was more about ritual than about caring for others. Indeed, many have pointed to the fact that this is the action that got Jesus killed, for he called for the temple to be a house of prayer for all people, opening the doors to those shut out from the worship of God. In this way, he challenged the religious system of first century Judaism that was structured around purity laws that shut people out from the worship of God, and he viewed the temple as that which symbolized the religious formalism of his day. Indeed, his actions in the temple signify his direct claim to speak and act with the authority of God, challenging those who set themselves up as God's authorities.

Jesus as God's Envoy

It is clear from reading the Gospels that in Jesus' experience of Israel's God, he felt a strong sense of vocation. He believed himself to be at the very least a prophet sent by God, but perhaps more importantly as God's envoy sent by God to proclaim the coming rule of God and to act in power in God's name against the forces of injustice. His mission was wholly connected to God, and as such, he believed he was acting by the authority of God, especially through his miracles.

The Gospels are replete with stories of Jesus performing miracles, mostly in efforts to heal and restore those suffering from a variety of maladies. Jesus' miracles were acted parables that give visual and tangible evidence of his proclamation that God's rule had come. His miracles were acts against the chaos, God's enemy that wreaked havoc on God's good creation. But they were also visual parables that brought God's judgment on a societal system that disregarded the needs of the most vulnerable. In healing and restoring those who suffered, Jesus was expressing God's compassion on all, affirming the goodness of human existence in God's good creation.

Jesus also seems to have understood that in following him, people were being obedient to God. In Mark 8:27-38, Peter, who misconceives what it means for Jesus to be the promised Messiah, confesses Jesus as the Messiah. In response, Jesus teaches that he will die. He calls all who want to become his disciples to take up the cross and follow him. He further defines discipleship as losing one's life for his sake and the sake of the gospel. The one who does this is promised salvation. Those who are ashamed of Jesus and his words, however, of them he will be ashamed when he comes in the glory of the Father. Thus, the faithfulness of the disciple in following Jesus demonstrates obedience to God.

So, it seems clear that Jesus understood his vocation to be to carry out God's mission to the world, and in doing so, Jesus served as the envoy and representative who ushered in the kingdom of God. While he certainly believed his mission was to be God's envoy, and he called others to follow him as he set forth God's new work,

Jesus remained wholly theocentric, and he often rejected the acclamations of divinity, preferring to view himself as the Son of Man.

Jesus the Human One

While many Christians affirm the divinity of Jesus, and while we could spend a great deal of time discussing whether Jesus claimed to be divine, or what the earliest followers believed about his divinity, or the events at the Council of Nicaea and the creed that came forth from that council meeting that defined the son as the same substance of the father, there is one important aspect of Jesus' nature that cannot be disputed. Jesus was human; as every bit as human as any person of his time. While many Christians today may prefer to see Jesus as divine, even to the extent that in our minds he is more divine than human, the historical reality and the theological depth of his humanity is something we must not overlook or downplay. Indeed, looking more closely at Jesus as a human is something that gives rich meaning to Jesus' life for Christian faith.

There are many titles that are used in the New Testament to describe Jesus, but the one title that Jesus preferred to use to refer to himself was "the son of man." This title has been hotly debated among scholars, but one thing seems to be certain. Jesus favored this as a reference for himself, and in doing so, he was using it as a way of declaring his identity with human existence. The phrase, son of man, is a term that simply means a human. Jesus was the son of man, the human one, or the one who embodied what it means to be human.

There are at least three important points that can be made from the observation that Jesus was human. First, to say that Jesus was human is to say that he had a body. This may be an obvious point to make, but making it demonstrates an important truth for us. If Jesus took on human flesh in the incarnation, then we must affirm that the essence of human flesh and human existence are good. This was the problem with many Christians in the early church beginning in the second and third centuries. They could not accept that Jesus was both divine and human, for perfect, transcendent divinity cannot take on imperfect and defiled flesh. Thus, they formulated ideas that Jesus was only a vision, but he could not have been a real human. Yet, this seems to be exactly what the New Testament teaches us about Jesus. The human body became the home of God. This raises significant theological questions, particularly concerning the idea that every person is born with an inherent sin nature. But to affirm Jesus as a human re-affirms the ancient Hebraic idea that all humans are made the image of God.

The second significant point to make about Jesus' humanity is that in being human, Jesus represents for us what it means to be faithful to God. Jesus was not programmed to follow God. He chose to follow God. And in faithfully following the ways of God, he became the paradigmatic disciple, who sets the example for others who seek faith in God and who seek to live God's will.

This is artfully communicated in Mark through the plot of the narrative that seems to hint that an early Christian audience might understand their own lives of discipleship as paralleling Jesus' life. An early Christian audience of Mark's narrative would have recognized the story of Jesus as their own story. From baptism, to proclaiming the kingdom of God and doing the will of God, to facing opposition, persecution, and death, one aspect of Mark's presentation of Jesus reflects the life of the Christian audience of Mark's narrative. In other words, the lives of Jesus' followers, if they are faithful disciples, should mirror his life.

But the third theological point taken from our observation that Jesus was human is that in taking on human existence, Jesus became vulnerable to human struggle, pain, and suffering. While affirming human existence as good, and while seeking to restore humanity to the original blessings of the creation, Jesus nonetheless faced the pain and suffering of human existence. Again, we can look to the plot of Mark, particularly how Mark handles the temptation of Jesus, to see this idea very clearly.

One interesting feature about the temptation of Jesus is that Mark's account is much shorter than either Matthew's or Luke's, both of whom include details that are absent from Mark. In only two verses, Mark raises challenging theological questions by what he does say as well as through what he does not say about Jesus' temptation. I don't have the space to rehearse all the explanations scholars propose as to why details are missing from Mark, or perhaps why Matthew and Luke felt it necessary to include details, but I can offer my own interpretation that gets at the heart of Mark's theology and offers us a way of seeing Jesus' humanity as our own.

In my view, the reason Mark's temptation story is shorter than Matthew's or Luke's is not because Mark was less concerned for details. The purpose is to imply to the hearers of his story that Jesus faced temptations and trials throughout his life, and not just in a one-time encounter with the mythical character Satan. Moreover, the shortness of Mark's account of Jesus' temptation also indicates to the readers that Satan was not the primary tempter of Jesus. Mark shows us through the remainder of his narrative that Jesus faced trials and temptations throughout his life, and most of these did not come from Satan, but from Jesus' closest followers, and even Jesus' own inner struggle, particularly in the garden on the night of his arrest.

Another interesting, but I think more theologically awkward trait peculiar to Mark's story of Jesus' temptation is the way Jesus is placed in the wilderness to be tempted. The opening chapter of Mark reaches a crescendo at the baptism of Jesus, when we hear the voice from heaven express God's pleasure with Jesus, and when the Spirit of God comes upon Jesus. Yet, immediately, to use one of Mark's favorite words, the same Spirit that came lovingly onto Jesus casts him into the wilderness to be tempted.

While both Matthew and Luke soften Mark's rawness by using a Greek word that indicates that the Spirit led Jesus into the wilderness, Mark is clear to use a term that communicates the idea that the Spirit of God threw Jesus into the wilderness for the explicit purpose of facing temptation. In other words, though he is proclaimed by God to be the Beloved Son, Jesus would not be protected from the vulnerability of being human. Indeed, it appears that Mark understands that God placed Jesus in the circumstance of temptation.

While the traditional interpretation says that Jesus had to face temptation to be the pure sacrifice for human sin, and thus God allowed him to be tempted, I think the more theologically rich interpretation is that God was intentionally putting God's future at risk. Jesus was not tempted just to know what humans face. Nor was he tempted as a way of making him the worthy sacrifice for our sins. By deliberately casting Jesus into the wilderness to be tempted, God was placing God's purposes in the hands of the human Jesus, taking the risky chance that Jesus might fail, thus exhibiting divine vulnerability in the human Jesus. And yes, it was entirely possible that Jesus could have failed, and thus we must admit that there is a great measure of scandal to God's providence in relation to the life of Jesus.

Although we tend to picture Jesus as a divine figure who had it all under control, the reality is that Jesus lived a very vulnerable life and was not immune to or protected from the challenges that the people of his time confronted every day, especially those persons at the bottom of the embedded social and religious structures of Palestine. First century Palestine was a volatile place within the Roman Empire, and those on the fringes of that society who were oppressed by injustice and violence were the most vulnerable to the pains and struggles of life.

But the idea that Jesus embraced human vulnerability raises a crucial theological question. For what reason did Jesus live as a human susceptible to the struggles of life? Did he become incarnate and face human vulnerability just so he could be a sacrifice for our sin? While many Christians answer this question with a resounding yes, it seems to me that there must be more to Jesus being human than just God's plan for him to become a sacrifice. Jesus' choice to take on human vulnerability was based on something more concrete that had a more intimate effect on those vulnerable persons around him. His free choice to be vulnerable to everyday existence was not for the purpose of being some sort of worthy sacrifice. His choice to take on human existence was a choice to unite with the most vulnerable of society.

The humanity of Jesus is theologically rich for our understanding of him and how he becomes the model for our own faith. As the paradigmatic disciple, Jesus expresses faith in God and faithfulness to God as he embodies the vulnerability of human existence. In doing so, Jesus does not walk aloof of the struggles and injustices of human life, but endures them with hope and faith. His life was indeed both radical and scandalous, but his hope in God and God's rule of justice that he sought to embody, caused him to embrace the radical and scandalous life to which God had called him, even though it would lead to a violent death.

Jesus and the Radical Rule of God

I recall growing up in church and always seeing various portraits of Jesus hanging on the walls. As a child, I assumed that Jesus was a white man with flowing locks of hair, who always wore a white robe and always had a look of calm on his face. More often than not, Jesus would be pictured with little children and young animals around him in a representation of peace and tranquility. A confrontational Jesus would never have crossed my mind.

But over the years that I have spent reading the Gospels, I have come to the conclusion that Jesus was a confrontational person, who was vastly concerned with the social injustices of his day. Jesus was not simply a teacher of spirituality as we like to make him out to be. Nor was he some divine figure who went about Galilee healing people. He was certainly both of these, but Jesus was also a political figure, whose words and deeds challenged the unjust political powers of his time.

This is not to suggest that Jesus was a politician in the way we think about politics today, nor is it to suggest that Jesus advocated a religious form of government. Such already existed in the ancient world as no known civilization existed apart from religion having an indivisible relationship with the state. Nor should we think of Jesus as seeking to involve himself in any political power system, whether the secular power of Rome or the religious power of the temple leadership. Indeed, we know very well that Jesus worked outside and in opposition to the standing power of both Roman authorities and the religious leadership of Jerusalem.

What I mean by saying that Jesus was a political figure is that his message and his mission confronted the social structures of his day with the politics of God. In other words, when we talk about Jesus, we need to take very seriously that Jesus' message was fraught with challenges to the politics of his day; his was a subversive politics. While eventually crucified in an act of cooperation between the two power centers he confronted, Jesus' teachings were not primarily about sin and salvation, heaven and hell. His central message was a new politic, a new way of existing in human society. His politics were the politics of compassion and justice, and central to his political message was his belief and his proclamation that God's kingdom was coming into the world; a kingdom that was a subversive revolutionary resistance to the Roman Empire and the religious ruling elite of Judaism.

Thus, instead of seeking worldly political power through violence, domination, and oppression, which Jesus and others witnessed first-hand from the Roman Imperial power, and instead of acquiescing with the practice of violence, domination, and oppression as the religious leaders of Israel did as a way of satisfying Rome enough to keep their places of religious power, Jesus called for a new politic, one that was shaped by the character and presence of God's rule and one that was manifested in the radical living of his disciples.[1]

While most scholars do agree that the central theme of Jesus' teaching was the rule of God, there is much disagreement about what Jesus meant by this term. Again, the scholarly debates on this issue are too complex for my purposes here. But, before we seek an answer to the question about what Jesus meant by the phrase "kingdom of God", it might be helpful first to dismiss assumptions we might have about the character of God's kingdom. In other

---

[1] The classic text on the politics of Jesus is John Howard Yoder's *The Politics of Jesus*. Various other scholars have approached Jesus as a political figure, including John Dominic Crossan and Marcus Borg.

words, these are the understandings we commonly have about the kingdom that are uninformed and incorrect.

First, the kingdom of God is not primarily a spiritual realm. It is spiritual in that it comes from God, but it is not heaven, as we might often think, and getting to some place called heaven is not the purpose of following Christ. Second, the kingdom of God is not primarily about personal spirituality. God's coming kingdom does transform us personally and in our Christian living we live as individuals who are in a personal relationship to God, but the kingdom of God cannot be reduced merely to personal spirituality.

What we need to understand about the meaning of the phrase, as Jesus used it, is that the term itself is politically charged. Jesus did not randomly pick this metaphor; he chose it as a challenge to the Roman imperial power that carried out injustice. He viewed the rule of God as coming into the word as the dynamic presence of God's love, compassion and justice. In calling people to enter the kingdom of God and follow him, Jesus was calling people to join an alternative empire, the Empire of God, over which God ruled and in which there was an alternative way of living in community with others.

What Jesus was doing through his ministry was calling people out of an existence that focused on the power of this world into a community over which God ruled as king. And he was calling them to offer their allegiance to God and not Caesar. This was the significance of confessing Jesus as Lord in the Roman Empire. Such a confession in the Roman world signified that one was no longer giving loyalty to Caesar or to the Roman system of domination, oppression, violence, and injustice. Confession of Jesus as Lord was not just a conversion experience in the way that we think of today as an individualized spiritual transformation; it was much more. Confessing Jesus as Lord was a transformation of the person from allegiance to one way living to another way of living. It was an act of insubordination against the so-called supremacy of the world's strongest power and an embrace of the call of Jesus to take up the cross and follow him. Joining the Jesus movement meant standing in opposition to worldly powers that carried out oppression, violence, and injustice.

Yet, the alternative kingdom Jesus was ushering into the world could not, in reality, face up to the power of Rome. Jesus and his followers were never significant challengers of Rome's military power, and Christians in the empire remained outsiders for centuries, and were, at various points, persecuted by the Roman authorities. In fact, joining the Jesus movement could quite possibly lead a person to death. From a worldly perspective, then, this Jesus movement, and Jesus' message about God's kingdom, would be seen as an inevitable failure. After all, was not the movement's leader put to death on a Roman cross? So how does the rule of God, which Jesus proclaimed as near, continue to come into the world, since the bearer of God's rule was put to death? God's kingdom continues to manifest itself in the world through the followers of Jesus who seek a different way of living and relating to others, both neighbors and enemies.

Jesus' Call to Radical Love

There is no doubt that Jesus commanded his followers to love their enemies. Moreover, there is no room for negotiation with Jesus on this point. No intelligent person can present a persuasive argument against taking his command seriously. Indeed, while we attempt to evade Jesus' clear teaching by placing limitations on his command, specifically related to who we love and how much we love, these limitations cannot be accepted by those who seek to follow the teachings of Jesus with great sincerity.

While loving one's enemy is a difficult and often impossible struggle, viewing Jesus' command as unattainable misses something deeply theological that is rooted in the heart of the gospel of grace. In our finite human existence, we believe that the strength to love others is found in ourselves and in our ability to muster up a forced love. We hear Jesus' command, believe it to be true, but grit our teeth and force what is humanly impossible to do; love someone who we believe to be unlovable. But such a view of Jesus' command will certainly lead us to fail.

The ability to love others, and especially our enemies, comes not from our own strength. Rather, we find the strength to love our enemies through the character and image of God that dwells in us, just as God dwelt in Jesus. In other words, our love for others comes not so much from our human capacity to love. It is only through God's empowering grace, given to us through God's limitless love, that we find the power to love others, even our enemies. Our strength to love others can only be discovered in our identity in Christ, as we are transformed by his call to see others as he sees others.

There are many good deeds that Jesus defined as actions of love, but there are some foundational actions that are at the core of his message that God loves the world. In fact, while many acts of goodness could be discussed, it seems to me that Jesus modeled for us four primary actions and reactions towards those who were his friends and enemies.

First, Jesus calls his followers to respond to the harm that is done to them with actions that are nonviolent. Jesus calls his followers to turn the other cheek when struck. When Jesus was arrested in the garden, the height of his conflict with his enemies, he responded with nonviolence and called his disciples to do the same. While those who came to seize him carried swords and clubs, Jesus reacted to their aggression with peacefulness. Thus, a reaction to a wrong done to us by our enemies that is both an authentic and transformative expression of Christ's love is always nonviolent.

This does not mean that Jesus forbade the seeking of justice. Rather, he envisioned seeking God's true justice that breaks a cycle of hatred and violence. Moreover, Jesus' command for his followers to turn the other cheek is not a command for them to become weak in the face of evil done against them. Rather, through turning the other cheek, Jesus' disciples expressed a strength that epitomizes the actions of Jesus and opens the possibility for love and peace between them and their enemies.

Second, Jesus commands love for enemies through unconditional forgiveness for the wrongs others have committed against them. God's forgiveness for humanity is not based on the human action of confession and repentance. God's forgiveness is unconditional and extends to those who have committed the most gravest of sins. Thus, if we are to reveal the character of God to others, then we must extend the same kind of forgiveness that God has so graciously extended to us.

Yet, forgiveness is not simply the overlooking of a wrong that has been committed. Those who commit wrongs against others and against society should be brought to justice. However, the justice we seek is not a condition for the forgiveness we are called to offer. In fact, the justice we seek must be restorative justice; a justice that offers reconciliation and a rebuilding of relationships. Jesus does not command forgiveness when someone serves their penalty for a wrong committed. Rather, he calls for forgiveness apart from that penalty, for he believed that forgiveness opens the opportunity for healing and transformation.

Third, the radical love for both neighbors and enemies to which Jesus calls us requires that we seek compassion and justice. Jesus' command to love your neighbor and enemy is also a call to seek justice as a part of love; justice that seeks to lift up. Indeed, love that does not express itself in justice towards all is not love. As John Dominic Crossan states, "Justice is the body of love, love the soul of justice. Justice is the flesh of love, love is the spirit of justice. When they are separated we have a moral corpse. Justice without love is brutality. Love without justice is banality"[1]

Fourth, Jesus' actions and words expressed love for enemies through the practice of welcoming and embracing enemies. We can look to Jesus' experience with Judas, the one who would betray him. Jesus remained in table fellowship with Judas to the very end; an act which served as an expression of hospitality and intimacy. Serving as host, Jesus not only shared a meal with Judas, he also washed the feet of his would be enemy. While Judas moved ahead with his evil intentions against Jesus, Jesus remained true to the character of God by continuing his hospitality and intimacy with

---

[1] John Dominic Crossan, *God and Empire: Jesus Against Rome, Then and Now.* (HarperCollins, 2008), 190.

Judas. Though Judas rejected Jesus, Jesus refused to reject Judas, and instead, he embraced and loved his enemy.

Moreover, the Parable of the Good Samaritan expresses the idea that love for enemies involves extending one's neighborly community to embrace friends and foes. Luke, the only evangelist to tell the parable, narrates that a man approached Jesus asking, "What must I do to inherit eternal life?" In response to the man's query, Jesus invites him to answer his own question by asking, "What is written in the law?" The man replies with theological accuracy, quoting what every Hebrew knew from childhood, that the law is summed up as a dual command to love God and to love one's neighbor. In response to the man's answer, Jesus affirms his orthodox statement and assures the man that if he does this he will indeed have eternal life.

The man's next question, "Who is my neighbor?" seems innocent at first, but since Luke tells us that the man was seeking to justify himself, we might presume that in asking the question, the man desired to limit his neighborly community. In other words, the man's real question might be, "Who am I required to love in order to gain eternal life?" It is this question that prompts Jesus to tell his shocking parable.

The parable is familiar enough to most of us not to retell it here, but a central question we might want to ask to get at the heart of the parable and why Jesus tells it the way that he does is to consider why Jesus chose a Samaritan as the unlikely hero of the story.

The Samaritans were considered by most Judeans as an inferior race. They were believed to be descended from Israelites who had intermarried with other nations after being exiled to Assyria in 722 B.C.E. While Samaritans claimed the Torah as their law, Judeans did not view them any better than they viewed Gentiles. In the minds of Judeans, Samaritans were half-breeds.

The shock and offensiveness of Jesus' parable, then, is that the unlikely hero of the story is not a racially pure Hebrew, but a member of a people believed to be lesser and impure. Indeed, the man is so shocked by this turn of events that in response to Jesus' question, "Which of these three do you think proved to be a neighbor to the man?" the man cannot even utter the word Samaritan, but simply replies, "The one who showed him compassion."

In response to the man's answer, Jesus commands, "Go and do likewise." Jesus is telling the man, "This Samaritan has set for you the example of what it is to be a neighbor to others, for he has widened his neighborly community to include someone who hates him and someone he has been taught to despise."

In showing compassion to someone from a race that despised his own, and one which I am sure he had been taught to hate, the Samaritan put away those prejudices that may have caused him to pass by like the priest and the Levite, and he widened his own conception of who was his neighbor. His generous act was more than a one-time act of compassion. His good deed reflected a deeper understanding of who he believed was a neighbor in his community.

There are those who would argue that the kind of love of which Jesus spoke and which he modeled is unattainable, whether on a personal or a communal level. They argue that love will not change the relationship. But this argument is theologically short-sighted, for if we believe that love is the prime characteristic of God, and that the love of God is powerful enough to change the world, and if we have embraced and now bear that love in our new identity in Christ, then we must believe that the love we share with others is the power through which God seeks to love and redeem all humanity, even our enemies.

Jesus' Call to Radical Living

Western Christianity has so focused on the individual before God that the communal nature of Jesus' call to a life of faith and practice has been all but lost. While we certainly see Jesus calling individuals to follow him in faithful discipleship, they are always called into the community of God's people in which they are to find a new way of existing in the world that demonstrates the ethics of God's rule. In one sense, the followers of Jesus formed somewhat of a political community who viewed themselves in opposition to that which was present in the outside world and culture of the Roman Empire.

Again, there was no way of challenging the Roman Empire on its own terms, and this way of thinking would not fit with Jesus' teachings about non-violence. But in forming an alternative political community that acted, in its own way, subversively to Rome, the early Christian community offered an ethic of living that was counter to what Rome stood for. In light of Jesus' teachings and his death on a Roman cross, this way of living became the norm for the community. But perhaps more importantly, this way of living was not an attempt to withdraw from the culture in which they lived. Rather it was a way of living that engaged and critiqued the cultural norms of the Roman world. There are some significant practices modeled or explicitly stated by Jesus that clarifies this radical way of living.[1]

Jesus called his followers to service, not political domination. Jesus serves as the paradigm of service as he claims to give his life for others (Mark 10:45). Moreover, in washing the disciples' feet, which was an act of humiliation equating himself to a house slave, Jesus modeled what it means to serve others. In doing so, he set forth the norm of living in community with others; a standard that reversed the importance of status within the new covenantal community.

The invasion of God's rule challenges the rule of unjust and oppressive power. Therefore, Jesus calls his followers to be a community in which imperial ideas of authority are cast out and replaced by a new ethic of service. Ironically, the political symbol of Roman power and domination, the cross, becomes for the followers of Jesus the symbol of service in the community, and the pattern of lordship practices found outside the community are to be replaced by the service demonstrated by the Son of Man, who gives his life as a ransom for the many (Mark 10:32-45). One who seeks to be great in the present rule of God, then, must become a servant of all (Mark 9:35; 10:43). Service in the present rule of God, then, is viewed as true greatness.

---

[1] Much of what follows originally appears in my essay, "'If Any Want to Become My Followers': Character and Political Formations via the Gospel of Mark" in *Character Ethics and the New Testament: Moral Dimensions of Scripture*. Robert L. Brawley, ed. (Westminster John Knox Press, 2007)

Jesus calls for inclusive welcoming, not exclusion based on status, as the norm of living in community. The discussion of who was the greatest among the twelve in Mark 9 prompts Jesus to take unto himself a child and declare that faithfulness to Jesus and to his God is found in the actions of welcoming a child. While we can take the child to mean literally a child, we may also view Jesus as using the child to represent those seen as weak or of lowly status. The language fits the idea of social welcoming and hospitality in the first century, which would have been extended to friends and family.[1]

Roman society, both in the Republic and then in the imperial period was built on a distinct class structure. Of course, wealth was an important factor in determining the class in which one found oneself. This strict system helped to maintain the practice of patronage, through which clients were held down. Moreover, this class structure prevented social mobility, which meant that the classes maintained a degree of pedigree and segregation, preventing social interaction between the classes, except when necessary.

Jesus rebuffs this standard of exclusion by declaring that the weakest of a society must find inclusion into the community of Jesus. The practice of such inclusion may have been shocking to new members, who may very well have struggled with letting go of their status over another within the new community. This is probably why Mark tells us the twelve were arguing over who was the greatest and why James and John are narrated as requesting seats of authority on the right and left of Jesus. These exclusive views may have reflected views held by some to whom Mark writes his Gospel. Yet, the norm of the community was one of inclusion, the welcoming of all that was not based on status.

This is illustrated in the life of Jesus himself as he welcomes the marginalized and as he institutes the community meal. Meals would certainly have served as symbols of exclusion as the menu of the wealthy was more elaborate and indulgent than that of the poor. Yet, in eating with tax collectors and sinners, Jesus was affirming

---

1 Bruce J. Malina & Richard L. Rohrbaugh, *Social Science Commentary on the Synoptic Gospels* (Minneapolis: Fortress Press, 1992), 237; Craig A. Evans, *Mark 8:27-16:20* (Dallas: Word, 2001), 62.

that the banquet of God's kingdom was open to all to come and partake. All would find equality and acceptance in the rule of God.

Jesus teaches his followers that the power of goodness, not oppressive power, is the norm for making and keeping peace. Jesus stated in the Beatitudes, "Blessed are the peacemakers." Peace and non-violence are the heart of Jesus' message and life, and he calls his followers to "be at peace with one another." But he commands that peace be made through the power of goodness.

Such a notion, however, is counterintuitive to a world system that seeks to find peace through oppression and war. The Roman Empire maintained the *Pax Romana*, the peace of Rome, only through the power of the emperor to exhort his legions upon the subjugated peoples of the Empire. Greatness was classified by power, and weakness and suffering were viewed as detriments to the honor, peace and unity of the Roman Empire.

Yet in Jesus' teaching, peace is not achieved through one being dominant over another. Violence begets more violence, as "an eye for an eye will only make the whole world blind," to quote Gandhi. Rather, in rejection of dominance, Jesus calls his followers to humble acts of service and goodness that are inherently non-violent. Resistance to evil is carried out more effectively through the non-violent reaction to aggression that can lead to restoration.

In the miracle story narrated in Mark 5:1-20, Jesus is confronted with an evil spirit that has possessed a man. When Jesus encounters this man, he asks for the name of the demon. The response the unclean spirit offers is "My name is Legion; for we are many." While the explicit meaning of the name expresses the idea that the man was possessed by more than one spirit, in the hearing of Mark's original audience there is something politically subversive in the use of the name that a first century audience would not miss.

The use of the name Legion in this story is the author's way of taking a direct slap at the supposed power of the Roman Empire; the Legions of military forces that enforced the infamous *Pax Romana*. This reference would not have been lost on the hearing of Mark's original audience and they certainly would have picked up on the meaning. Thus, while the miracle stands as a testimony to the power of Jesus over the demonic and the healing he offered to those possessed, it also functions in Mark's story as a judgment against the imperial power that Rome executed through military strength. Jesus understood that the power of goodness, which is the power of non-retaliation and non-violence, was the only power that could and would bring restoration and peace.

Jesus commanded the sharing of possessions in community, not self-indulgence and prosperity, as the economic norms of the community. Jesus' encounter with the rich man who seeks eternal life in Mark 10:17-22 serves as instruction on the use and possession of worldly goods in the community of Jesus. The man desires eternal life and, upon hearing Jesus state the commandments, which he claims to have kept, the man assumes that all is well. Yet Jesus calls him to live out his faith by selling his many possessions and giving the money to the poor. A choice he cannot make.

The story does not reveal how this man came about his wealth. We do not even know he is wealthy until he walks away (Mark 10:22). So why does Jesus pick this man to issue this demand? Perhaps this man has gained his possessions through some form of oppression of others. More certainly we can assume that he has neglected caring for others by hoarding his wealth, much like we can assume about the rich fool in the parable Jesus tells in Luke 12:13-21. Both will not relinquish their control over their abundance so that they might share with those who do not have.

Wealth in the Roman Empire was normally viewed as the ticket to power, particularly political power. The wealthy classes, senatorial and equestrian, used their wealth to gain and keep their political power. It is well known among historians that Julius Caesar went into huge debt as he pursued political power that eventually lead to his being emperor. Moreover, because of their fortune, the rich viewed themselves as superior to the lower classes in intelligence and ethical conduct.[1] In opposition to this Roman cultural norm, Jesus called his followers to relinquish control over their wealth and give it to the community to be used to care for those

---

1   J.A. Shelton, *As the Romans Did: A Sourcebook in Roman Social History* (New York: Oxford University Press, 1988), 10.

in need. Joining the Jesus movement demanded a renunciation of one's wealth as a tool of power and position and called for Jesus' followers to sell "their possessions and goods" and to give "to anyone as he had need" (Acts 2:45).

It is clear from reading the Gospels that Jesus set forth and modeled a way of living that is contrary to what has been and still is often the dominant world view. In doing so, Jesus' teachings were not so much focused on the personal salvation and spirituality of a person, but upon how a person lived in this world, particularly in community with others. Calling followers to a radical way of living politically, Jesus was calling them to something that was indeed costly.

The Cross of Jesus

The Gospels narrate their stories as if Jesus knew he would be put to death by the Roman authorities. In fact, the plot of each Gospel is focused on Jesus' travel toward the time and place of his crucifixion. Some have even suggested that the Gospels are passion narratives with introductions tacked on to them. Mark contains at least three specific statements made by Jesus about his future death and other implications from Jesus about his fate (8:31; 9:31; 10:33-34). While the author offers a backward looking theological interpretation of the sayings of Jesus, we can be sure that Jesus did understand that he would most likely be crucified. History had told him that to challenge the authority of Rome was treason, and the penalty for treason was death. He knew full well that as he progressed in his challenge against the authorities, both of the Jewish religious elite and the Roman Empire, he would be put to death as a rebel, just like hundreds of others.

But the classic text that interprets Jesus death as the example for his followers in the way they live in the world is Mark 8:34, where the author puts on the lips of Jesus, 'If any want to become my followers, let them deny themselves and take up their cross and follow me." This was and hopefully still is the mantra of what it means to follow Jesus. Indeed, it should be the creed that supersedes all creeds.

Our interpretation, however, must not simply be a spiritualizing of what Jesus says, as is common practice among many Christians. To do so would move too far away from the meaning of Jesus' statement that it becomes unrecognizable. Rather, our interpretation should be one that appropriates the declaration to our modern context while at the same time remaining connected to the original intent of the definition, and particularly to the interpretation of early Christians.

We know that the cross was a symbol of Roman tyranny, and that crucifixion was practiced by the Romans on many who were considered enemies of the state. Jesus was far from the only one killed on a cross, and far from the only innocent one who suffered this fate. Thus, in the context of Roman jurisprudence, Jesus was just another enemy of the state that needed to be silenced.

But the earliest followers of Jesus reflected on his death and reached a different understanding of the image of the cross. Though the cross was still a ruthless tool in the hands of an oppressive government, for the disciples, the cross had shifted from an external symbol of Roman tyranny to an internal symbol of faithfulness for the Christian community. For these earliest Christians, the cross served symbolically as the norm of a community that existed in a world not yet submissive to the rule of God. The cross became symbolic of the internal ethic of the community and the social formation of that community in opposition to Roman power. The symbol of the cross represented for them a new way for being human; one in which the virtues of Christ served to form a counter-cultural movement.

In the fourth century, however, for the Roman Emperor Constantine, the sacred symbol of Christ, the *Chi-Rho*, became the symbol of earthly power and might. In essence, a second shift took place that moved the understanding of the cross as a symbol of selfless discipleship to one by which to conquer through domination, oppression, and violence. Christianity, then, moved from the marginalized alternative community of discipleship to the dominant symbol of power in the West.

In our modern political environment, the religious conservative movement of the last three decades has once again led to a shift in the story of Jesus and the cross. The cross has become once more a symbol of political power, and the church has been swept into being part and parcel of one political agenda. Those entrapped by this movement view the cross at a distance, preferring to see it as only an object on which Jesus died for our sins, rather than taking the cross as their own and seeing it as the symbol of vulnerability and openness.

It is time for another shift, one that leads us back to the early Christian understanding of the cross as the power of God, and not the power of humans. Shifting our understanding of the cross back to how early Christians viewed the cross would lead the church to find afresh its identity as an alternative community in which individuals are not formed by power, greed, exclusion, and self-interests, but are shaped by the norms of Jesus and his cross.

Jesus' Call to Costly and Liberating Discipleship

Jesus' call to enter the rule of God by taking up the cross and following him calls for a radical new approach to life and living. Yet, we can often look at the demands Jesus voices in the Gospels with great trepidation, knowing that these are often too difficult for us to follow. Perhaps we are much like the folks in Mark 3:21, thinking Jesus has "gone out of his mind." Indeed, the church and individual Christians have ignored Jesus' radical teachings preferring to find spiritual fulfillment in a personal relationship with Jesus that is based solely on Jesus being our savior. Taking up the cross, renouncing possessions, loving and serving our neighbors and enemies, all seem too stringent and costly for us. We want the Jesus who calls us to salvation, but we reject the Jesus that demands discipleship. Yet, the irony of following Jesus is that though it is costly, it is at the same time, liberating.

In *The Cost of Discipleship*, Dietrich Bonhoeffer states very powerfully that grace cannot be cheap. "Cheap grace is grace without discipleship." Bonhoeffer coined an almost paradoxical phrase to describe the experience of salvation and discipleship: costly grace. In his words, costly grace is "costly because it costs a man his life, and it is grace because it gives a man the only true life." Bonhoeffer sees the call to follow Jesus as a call that is both costly and liberating.

In the Gospels, we find Jesus calling those who would become his followers. In the first chapter of Mark's story, Jesus calls two sets of brothers, all of whom are fishermen. He calls them to leave their nets, to leave their families, and to follow him. In this story, and other call stories, we discover the tension that Bonhoeffer points out as that which epitomizes the gospel: Discipleship is both costly and liberating.

When Jesus comes upon these fishermen they are doing what they normally do on any given day; they are fishing. Indeed, this was their life; this was their existence. Fishing was what was routine and comfortable for them. While their occupation as fishermen was hard work that brought many challenges, it is what they knew and it is who they were. Yet, when Jesus calls them, he calls them to leave their lives as they know them. He calls them to turn away from their normal existence and to let go of what they know best. How costly is such a decision?

While leaving fishing may not seem big to us, let's take into account what Jesus demands from another. A rich man approached Jesus wanting to know how he might gain eternal life. Jesus told him to keep the greatest commandments; to love God and to love others. Jesus then told the man, "Sell all your possessions and give to the poor." At this demand, the man turned away, refusing to accept the cost.

We must be careful not to distance ourselves too much from this story. In calling us to follow him, Jesus always demands that we relinquish our claims; our claims of independence, our claims to security and freedom, our claims to what we own, and our claims to live our lives as we see fit. To answer the call of discipleship is always costly. If it is not, it is not discipleship.

Yet, even as we speak of discipleship as costly, we must also view it as liberating. The call to the two sets of brothers to leave what they know, what gave them comfort and security, is at the same time a call to find liberation and hope in something that is transformative. While their lives of fishing certainly gave them a sense of normality, they were unknowingly missing what authentic life with God was like. Jesus' call for them to leave their nets and follow him was a call to embrace a new liberating existence.

But to accept the call of Jesus to follow him, we must relinquish what holds us back from the true gospel and what prevents us from becoming authentic disciples of Jesus. We must count the cost of discipleship, and we must be willing to move from our status quo existence of comfort, security, and that which we know as normal, to embrace the life changing, world transforming, and liberating power of the gospel. This is authentic discipleship that is both costly and liberating.

Does the Real Jesus Offend Us?

Yet, as the subtitle of a book puts it, many Christians view themselves as God-blessed, but never consider the fact that we are Christ-haunted.[1] We gather in worship of God, offering praise for God's love for us and God's blessings on us, but we often fail to heed Jesus' command to discipleship and radical living. From our places of blessing, we like to point our pious fingers at those outside, and even some inside the church and condemn them for their sins, while at the same time holding onto an understanding of God that is so far away from Jesus' life and teachings. In this way we create a God in our own image, in our own likeness, one that we can manage and one that is worshiped at churches where, as one of my kids puts it, "you can get an easy 'A'."

But this is not what it means to be a follower of the Jesus of the Gospels. Yes, following Jesus is liberating, but it is demanding, it is costly. Yet, the demands are too much for most of us, and we prefer a different Jesus who marches to the beat of our drum. But this is not the real Jesus, the biblical Jesus. For the real Jesus offends us.

When I was working on my Ph.D. in Edinburgh, Scotland, I would often take breaks from my writing and roam Auld Reekie,

---

1 David Dark, *The Gospel According to America: A Meditation on a God-blessed, Christ-haunted Idea*, Westminster / John Knox / 2005

as Edinburgh is affectionately known. One of my favorite places of respite from the grind of writing a dissertation was the National Gallery of Scotland. There I could view in peace the creative works from the great artists of history. It was there that I discovered one of my favorite paintings; one which I had only known from books. That painting is El Greco's *Savior of the World*.

For me El Greco's painting captures the essence of Jesus. Although El Greco painted a Jesus who looks more like one of El Greco's contemporary Europeans than a Jew living in first century Palestine, once you get past this historical flaw, you begin to appreciate what the artist has done. As I would sit there viewing this work, the face of the subject always drew me to himself. El Greco's Jesus is inviting, compassionate, and loving.

Yet, as I would sit for periods of time staring into the warm and compassionate face of the painted Savior, I would begin to see something else. Those same inviting and loving eyes became piercing and condemning. That once warm face now became offensive to me as if he was looking deep into my soul and witnessing the worst of human sin.

In Mark 6, Jesus, Nazareth's own hometown boy, returns home to preach to those who knew him as a child. You can imagine the anticipation they felt for what he might say as he preached his first sermon in his home synagogue. Yet, although Mark does not tell us the words that Jesus spoke, he does tell us that those who heard him "took offense at him" (Mark 6:3). Taken literally, they were scandalized by what he said. Why?

Perhaps they assumed that their hometown boy would make them proud by affirming their righteousness, their place as God's elect people, and their pious religious observances. Perhaps they assumed that Jesus would side with them against their enemies, preach stirring sermons convicting others of their sins and pointing to his own people as examples of what it means to live holy lives. Perhaps Jesus would tell them how God-blessed they really were. Whatever Jesus said in the synagogue on that day convinced the Nazarenes that the returning hometown boy was not the Jesus they wanted. Instead he was the Jesus they got; and they were offended.

We can look at this story and scornfully judge these people and others who reject Jesus, shaming them for not embracing the person and words of Jesus. But are we not just looking into the mirror at our own faces? Was not their problem with Jesus the same as our problem with Jesus? We embrace the Jesus we want, but we quickly reject the Jesus we get; the real Jesus who offends us.

The Jesus we want is our friend. He is our ally in the face of our enemies. This Jesus is always on our side, answering our prayers and blessing us. This Jesus tells us what we want to hear, makes us comfortable, and looks pleasingly at our self-righteousness. This Jesus is the one who applauds our hate speech and intolerance of others, who approves of our use of violence and war against our enemies, and who promises us that our capitalistic pursuits will bring us prosperity.

The Jesus we want is created in our own minds and answers to our demands. He permits us to wage unjust violence against our enemies in the name of national security. He allows us to hoard money and possessions in the name of financial security. He consents to our prejudices against people of other races, genders, religions and sexual orientations in the name of cultural security. Yes, this is the Jesus we prefer. He is the Jesus we can accept and worship.

But this is not the real Jesus. The real Jesus is the one who calls us to turn the other cheek, to love our enemies, to sell all we have and give to the poor, and to take up the cross and follow him. This is the Jesus who calls us to reach out to others and cross the boundaries of race, religion, culture, gender, and sexual orientation. This is the Jesus that dined with tax collectors, beggars, diseased, and various persons of questionable social standing. This is the Jesus who compels us to repent of our insular lives and to commit ourselves to work for justice, peace, and hope in our world. This is the Jesus who calls us to rethink our theological assertions and to open ourselves to being moved by his Spirit. And this is the Jesus, who being so offensive and so scandalous to his contemporaries, that he was crucified on the most offensive and scandalous instruments of Roman power-the cross. Yes, this is the radical Jesus, the scandalous Jesus, and the offensive Jesus; but he is the real Jesus, the biblical Jesus, and the Jesus who calls us out of sin into the salvation of radical discipleship. This is the Jesus we must reclaim.

Questions for Reflection and Discussion

1. In what ways did Jesus' experience of God influence his life and ministry?

2. How does viewing Jesus as a vulnerable human have an impact on our understanding our own humanity?

3. Why do we tend to emphasize what we believe about Jesus more than obeying what Jesus says?

4. When was the last time you heard a sermon on loving your enemies, giving up your possessions, seeking peace through non-violence, or any other command Jesus gives that calls for radical living?

5. How is following Jesus in faithful discipleship both costly and liberating?

6. Does Jesus offend you? If not, why not?

 Reclaiming the Church's Mission

I like your Christ. I do not like your Christians. Your Christians are so unlike your Christ.
                              -Mohandas Gandhi

I live in that region of the United States that has been dubbed the Bible belt; that southern part of the country where religion is as American as apple pie or as southern as fried chicken. Indeed, I live in a very religious community where there are a plethora of churches, prayers before meals even in non-religious settings, and where you can even go into a local fast food restaurant where they have Bible verses on their receipts, and every to-go bag gets a pamphlet on how to avoid hell and get into heaven. In the county in which I live, there are over 100 churches of various denominations and various sizes. Although all of them are part of the wider Christian tradition, which is unfortunate for it makes us somewhat monolithic in our religious understanding, this variety of places of Christian worship offers the seeker a selection of Christian theological beliefs, church polity, types of worship, and choices of dress. You really can't go wrong in finding a house of worship that fits what you want, unless of course you are not Christian. I know there are towns like this all over America.

Yet, despite the plethora of houses of worship in towns across this country, it seems to be that the church is becoming less relevant to the lives of people both within and outside the church. While many stay away from church for various reasons, many do cite the fact that the church is out of touch with their needs, that the church is too dogmatic and strict in its beliefs, and that for the most part it has sided with a particular political agenda. It is probably accurate to say that many folks stay away from church because they just don't find it worthwhile, and thus they do find excuses to stay away. But the fact of the matter is that these accusations against the church, as well as plenty of others, are often valid.

Moreover, among the folks who faithfully attend church Sunday after Sunday hoping to hear a word from God, are those who leave the place of worship with a great measure of dissatisfaction. Part of this dissatisfaction has to do with the person who comes to worship, whose life is filled with distractions that draw their attention and energy from focusing on God in worship. But much of this disappointment happens because the church has waned in its relevancy to touch people's lives and to translate the gospel for the needs of today's world. It is these people that find the church very ineffectual in its proclamation, hiding behind a spiritualism that is based on worship as entertainment and preaching as superficial. At church we are encouraged to allow our emotions to soak in the shallow songs that appear on the screen and the sermons that reinforce our beliefs, but we become uncomfortable when these challenge our status quo existence as people who choose comfort over vulnerability and prosperity over sacrifice.

But more tragically, we are discouraged from asking serious questions about faith and about the issues we face in our world, or we are given pat answers to these questions. In fact, we are encouraged to shut down our minds in church, which leads me to believe that church can often be one of the most intellectually dishonest institutions we can find. As I noted in the previous chapter, church is, as one of my kids said, "The place where you can get an easy 'A'."

We cannot equate relevancy with emotional manipulation and easy "A" theology. Folks don't want to come to church to have their emotions manipulated or to hear rehearsed answers to their questions. People who come to church come there to find meaning for their lives and relationships that are welcoming and embracing, not condescending. And while many churches may claim to be welcoming, the reality is that they are not welcoming those they judge as sinful.

Furthermore, people who come to church don't seek sermons that are mundane repetitions of outdated theology or unsophisticated platitudes. They want to be challenged by the gospel and how to follow Jesus in faithful discipleship. They want to deal honestly with deep questions about God, humanity, and the issues we face in our world. They want to hear that the gospel can change the world, but not simply through getting people saved, which is far removed from the central message of Jesus. People want to hear, indeed they need to hear, that Jesus' message is not about heaven or hell, but about living justly and faithfully here in this life.

That being said, there is no doubt that there are faithful and relevant churches all across this nation and this world. Faithfulness and relevance, however, cannot be equated with size. How many members a church has or how many baptisms a church performs is not the measure of faithfulness. In fact, there are many small churches that are probably more faithful to the call of Jesus than those mega-churches who have gone into tremendous debt to build elaborate places of worship and family life centers, but only present a false sense of relevancy.

Is it possible to reframe our understanding of Christian community that is more faithful to the Jesus of the Gospels? I am hopeful that it is. But any move in this direction must call for deep soul searching that deals seriously with the mission to which Jesus called his followers.

Jesus Called Followers, Not an Institution

How on earth did a movement involving a rugged band of first century Jewish peasants eventually become the largest institutional religion in the world? How did the followers of Jesus move from meeting in homes to building extravagant cathedrals, worship centers, and family life buildings? How did the preaching of the gospel move from being a prophetic ministry of calling people to faithful discipleship to being a multibillion dollar business that promises blessing, prosperity, and victory over our enemies? How did a once inclusive community that welcomed Jew and Gentile, male and female, slave and free, become an exclusive institution that works at its best to shut people out? How did a people called to weep and mourn create an atmosphere of worship that entertains and manipulates the emotions but does not call us to follow Jesus? How did the broken body of Jesus become an instrument of religious power?

Historians can debate these questions and can point to various times, events, and people that caused the growth and shifts of the church, for the good or the bad, and certainly we can learn from studying church history to see where things have gone wrong. But the question becomes for those of us who love Jesus and his church, "Can we ever recover what was lost? Can we ever reclaim the church as that which Jesus intended?" I have faith that we can.

Although I have become wary of the church as an institution, I have not given up entirely on the church as those who seek to follow Jesus. This includes both individuals and churches. But I am becoming more alarmed at the superficiality of the church as it seeks to bring in more and more people without calling them to live faithfully as followers of Jesus. I am particularly alarmed at the focus these churches place on the middle class, treating church like a product they want middle class professionals to buy. These churches seem to be nothing more than social clubs that provide members, if you can call them that, with a variety of activities, and they treat their members as if the church should be the center of their lives. Moreover, in order to keep them coming, worship in these churches is geared toward lifting our spirits each week, without causing us to reflect on how we can authentically follow Jesus. The focus is mostly on how to have a better prayer life, how to face our struggles, how to bring more people to church, and how to develop the relationship between me and Jesus, telling us that God has a word for each of us.

Perhaps I am overly skeptical of the church, and perhaps I am making a categorical fallacy by projecting what I have witnessed in my experience onto the larger church. I am aware that this may be true, but I am also aware that what I am pointing out is a reality in many churches. Thus, the question becomes, how do we reclaim the church as the followers of Jesus? Is it possible? Can the church return to its true purpose and existence in the world? I believe that it can, but I do think it will take an awful lot of questioning to peel back two millennia of institutional film that prevents us from finding our identity as followers of the crucified Jesus.

The Broken Body of Jesus, Not the Powerful People of God

Perhaps the most prominent metaphor to describe the church comes from the Apostle Paul's description of the church as the body of Christ, particularly his exegesis of the metaphor in 1 Corinthians 12. Paul's selection of this metaphor was not haphazard, for the image is so closely related to the center of Christian faith that the sign and that which it signifies cannot be easily distinguished. Indeed, the image of the church as the body of Christ signifies that the church is indeed the incarnation of Jesus in the world. The church is the mouth, the hands, the feet, and the heart of Jesus to a world in need of prophetic voices, serving hands and feet, and hearts of compassion. Yet, we have forgotten that Jesus' body was broken for us, and as such, the body of Christ in the world today should also be broken.

Henri Nouwen wrote, "It is often difficult to believe that there is much to think, speak or write about other than brokenness."[1] Brokenness, like many other terms that fit within its semantic domain, conjures up images of weakness and failure; images that for some reason we have taken to be far from what it means to be followers of Jesus. Yet, for some odd reason, we are particularly guilty of assuming that all things should work out for us. We pray to avoid struggle and pain, and in some sections of the church, we are told that if we have enough faith we can avoid these things and we can even become rich.

But, as followers of Jesus, why should we assume that our lives should be any less tragic than his own? This is certainly not to say

---

1 *Life of the Beloved: Spiritual Living in a Secular World* (New York, Crossroad, 1992), 73.

that we should be looking for suffering, as I think some often do. But we must be reminded that Jesus, the one we follow, suffered real evil, real pain, and real death. His human existence is not a story of victory, but one of brokenness that has meaning for our own humanity. Brokenness means that we become and remain vulnerable in our human existence, both as individual followers of Jesus and as the collective body of Christ. Despite the false teachings that Christians are blessed, or as we often like to say in an attempt to separate ourselves from others, "we are forgiven," Christians have no pride of place in God's creation, and thus, followers of Jesus must embrace brokenness as a faithful way of existing in the world both as individual followers of Jesus and as the collective body of Christ.

While Christianity has traditionally believed in a God who is all powerful, when I reflect on the life of Jesus, I am inclined to believe that the traditional view of God does not seriously consider the vulnerability of human existence as represented in Jesus' life and tragic death. Moreover, by coupling the belief that God is all-powerful with the idea that we, as opposed to others, are the blessed and chosen people of God, we mock the cross of Jesus. At no point in his life did Jesus ever suggest that we will be prosperous and secure if we only have faith in God.

Indeed, the church exists in the world as the suffering body of Christ that engages with the pains and struggles of those seeking hope, healing, redemption, and restoration. Jesus took on human brokenness in order to be intimate with those who struggled and suffered in this life. He did not separate himself from pain and brokenness, but he embraced it as a way of being intimate with those who suffer. His compassion was not a feeling of sympathy for the plight of the hurting, while he remained distant from their hurting. His compassion was the force that led him to be intimately bound to those who hurt.

If the church is ever to return to Jesus' vision for his followers, then those who claim to be Christian must choose to take up the cross of Jesus by choosing to be broken. Being a Christian does not remove our connectedness to the rest of humanity. Rather, following Jesus leads us to be more intimately connected to humanity, especially to humans who are broken. The body of Christ does not exist separate from the world, but lives in solidarity with the world as the broken body of Christ incarnate and suffering with the rest of humanity.

Prophetic Voice, Not Political Power

Part of the problem for the institutional church in America has been its quest for political power. Fundamentalist and conservative Christians have joined forces in an attempt to bring about political change that they believe will return America back to God. In other words, while many would not use the term, they would like to see America become something that resembles a theocracy. They envision a nation that is ruled by their brand of Christianity, which is actually a dangerous mixture of Christian superiority with American exceptionalism and prosperity. Yet, the history of the relationship between the church and the rule of the state cannot be overlooked as a warning sign that must be heeded. Perhaps it's time for a history lesson.

It was not unheard of that ancient civilizations considered religion as a major force in politics and government. Indeed, when Augustus, the most powerful Emperor of the Roman Empire, claimed the title of *pontifex maximus*, or high priest of Roman religion around 12 B.C.E., he solidified his role as both religious and political leader of the Roman Empire. In doing so he established the Imperial Cult of Rome and was able to use religion as a powerful force to maintain his rule. What Augustus did was not new and was not the last time a ruler took on the trappings of divinity. Indeed, many rulers of ancient civilizations fused religion and politics together in a claim to have the divine right to rule.

For the most part Rome remained a polytheistic culture, with people paying homage to many gods. Yet, in the year 313 C.E., Roman Emperor Constantine, after he had seized power over the Empire, issued the Edict of Milan. This decree, which came as a result of Constantine believing that the Christian God had given him victory over his enemy, and thus sole power in the Empire, reversed the persecution that had been sporadically carried out against Christians. Up to that point, though Christianity was growing and spreading, it was still on the margins of society and Christians were persecuted in local skirmishes with those who believed that the worship of one God was preposterous, and the persecutions of emperors like Nero (54-68 C.E.) and Diocletian (284-305 C.E.). Yet, by issuing the Edict of Milan, Constantine legalized Christianity, giving it primacy in the religiously eclectic Empire. Once a religion on the margins of society, Christianity grew in power after Constantine's edict, until it eventually became the only official religion of the Empire when Emperor Theodosius (378-395 C.E.) outlawed all other pagan religions. At this point, the church and the state were fused together into a dangerous alliance.

This entangled relationship continued during the Medieval Period, when crown and cross were virtually inseparable. During this period, institutional Roman Catholic Christianity was the only religion of Europe, and salvation was only found in the church and people were not allowed a choice of whether to be Christian or not, except for those Jews living in Europe who were often persecuted and blamed for the ills of society, especially the Black Plague. For over a millennium, church and state were indivisible, and loyalty to one was loyalty to the other. While there were points at which secular rulers and religious rulers were at odds with one another, the might of the state was often used to enforce religious doctrines and practices and to weed out heretics.

In 1517 Martin Luther challenged the authority of the Roman Church in what is known as the Protestant Reformation, a period of religious, political, and social upheaval that eventually led to schisms in the church, giving birth to different churches across Europe. Most of these movements found support from secular authority, Luther's included. Indeed, the Reformation of the church in England was very much a move by King Henry VIII against the papal authority of Rome, when Henry convinced the English Parliament to declare him head of the Church of England. Despite some radical movements in the Reformation, such as the Anabaptist movement that preached the separation of church and state, for the most of Europe the two powers remained entangled in an uneasy relationship, which led to the various religious wars of the sixteenth and seventeenth centuries.

A new experiment, however, was on the horizon as many who sought to escape religious persecution in Europe made their way to the New World. When the United States won its independence from England and established its own sovereignty, it was created as a nation that officially separated church and state, offering religious freedom to all its citizens. While there is no doubt that the Christian religion played a major role in the establishment of the United States, most of the founders embraced Enlightenment Deism. Yet, they did consider themselves to be Christian, and thus, it is historically accurate to say that the Christian religion helped to shape this new nation.

Nevertheless, it is wrong to assume that America was created as a Christian nation, as many would claim today. Yet, in our increasingly antagonistic political culture, some religious leaders and some politicians would like to see a blurring of the lines between church and state. For example, the religious broadcaster and onetime presidential candidate, Pat Robertson once stated, "The ideal society is one in which church and state are inseparable." His dream would be to establish a Christian nation, and he is not alone in dreaming this. It seems that these leaders do not know their history, or they choose to ignore this history.

While history has proven that such an alliance is very dangerous, there are significant theological reasons why church and state must remain separate. First, as followers of Jesus, we must remember that we are primarily citizens of the kingdom of God and not the kingdom of our country. Jesus has called us first and foremost to pledge allegiance to him and his teachings. Our allegiance to the state, and its symbols, is secondary to our faithfulness to God's rule. This does not mean that we cannot be good citizens of both, for Christians are called to be salt and light in the world. Moreover, our faith means that we are not called to separate ourselves from living as humans in this world and we must be involved in civic engagement working across religious divisions for justice and the common good. But our ultimate loyalty must be to the life and teachings of Jesus, particularly his call for justice and peace for all people, and especially toward the marginalized of our society. Therefore, when the state makes economic policies that are unjust for the weak and poor, the church must speak and call for justice. When the state limits the rights of segments of a population, the church must stand for equality and inclusion. When the state creates foreign policies that lead to war, the church must stand for peace. But we can only do this when we remain at a prophetic distance from the state.

Second, the biblical story teaches us very clearly that God has sought to bless the world, the entire cosmos, long before the birth of America. The Christian faith extends beyond the boundaries of America to the far reaches of our globe. This is one reason why worship spaces should not include patriotic symbols such as the American flag, and worship services should not incorporate patriotic themes and songs, for the gospel is for all people. This is not to suggest that we should not be thankful to God for what we have in this country, but we need to worship God as the God of all people and not the God of American religion. If we only acknowledge God as blessing America, then we fail to recognize the vastness of God's love and God's will and purpose to redeem all humanity, and we set America up as vital to God's will and purpose for the world, which is heresy.

History has demonstrated that the relationship between the church and the state is hazardous. If the state is under the control of the church, then religious freedoms will be lost, as one religion will seek to control the state. Likewise, if the church becomes a mechanism of the state, then the church cannot stand at a prophetic distance from which it can speak to any unjust and abusive policies of the state. Those Christians who would like for America to become a Christian nation are reaching for nostalgic period in this nation that never truly existed, and if it ever does, we will find ourselves repeating the bloody past relationship between church and state.

Bearing Witness to Jesus, Not Condemning Sinners

What then is the purpose of being a witness of Jesus? Christianity has always sought new believers, following the missionary character of Israel's God and the commands of Jesus. My view of Christianity's relationship to other religions is not necessarily mutually exclusive to a belief in the missionary purposes of the church, as long as we have a proper understanding of evangelism. After all, I cannot deny the call to mission that is explicit in the Christian Bible. But my understanding of mission and evangelism has changed over the years, partly due to my reading closely the stories of Jesus, and partly due to my distaste for methods used by those who define bearing witness to Jesus as condescending arm-twisting.

I often numbingly flip through the channels late at night, stopping at times to listen to religious broadcasting, which is seldom any good. My interest in doing this is only partly religious. Mostly I want to see what theological nutcase was saying what in the name of God. One night I ran across a program featuring Kirk Cameron. Cameron is probably most famously known as Mike, the teenage son on *Growing Pains*, a popular TV sitcom of the mid-80s. Cameron is better known today, however, for his zealous Christian ideas and his association with Ray Comfort, an evangelist who, with Cameron, seeks to convert people to Christianity.

Both Cameron and Comfort call what they do witnessing. It seems to me, however, that while they may be passionate about what they are doing, and they certainly believe they are right in doing it, they are more than anything being confrontational and condemning to the extent that they may do more harm than good. Their approach is certainly not new, for many Christians consider this kind of proselytizing as being faithful to Jesus' commission for his followers to go into the world and share the gospel with all people. I don't doubt the passion of those who believe in this kind of evangelism, and I don't necessarily want to judge the motivations of the hearts of folks like these. But I am concerned that this kind of witnessing, and the zeal that seems to fuel it, is misguided and may not be what Jesus envisioned when he voiced the command for his followers to be his witnesses.

For too long we have believed certain misconceptions that have been energized by our zeal to be what we believe to be faithful to Jesus' call for us to be his witnesses. I would like to identify a few of these misconceptions in order to lay the ground work for what I think is a more faithful definition and description. These are beliefs and strategies that many have practiced in their efforts at evangelism that do not, in my mind, reflect Jesus' own practice and instruction. Indeed, while these may have limited success in converting people to the Christian religion, they may do more harm to the church's witness of Jesus.

Misconception No. 1: Witnessing is converting people to the Christian religion. This is simply not true for a number of reasons, but two are crucial for us to understand. First, we do not convert people; only God can change the hearts and minds of people. Our Bible thumping arguments, though we think they are eloquent, do not convert people. Second, nowhere does Jesus say for us to convert people to our religion. He says to share the good news and to call people to follow him, to follow his radical way of living, but he does not call us to convert people to our religion or to our theological doctrines.

Misconception No. 2: Witnessing is telling people they are morally corrupt without God. First of all, human morality is not dependent on humans believing and following God. People can certainly be moral people without being religious and without believing in God. As well, many people who claim to be Christian have demonstrated that they are not very moral. Second, witnessing is not convincing people that they are sinners. I have heard many purported experts in witnessing say that in order to get people saved, you must first convince them they are morally corrupt sinners. The problem with this is that the gospel is not about condemning people, it is about showing compassion. Moreover, this position assumes that Christianity is morally superior to other religions and the non-religious.

Misconception No. 3: Witnessing is convincing people that Christianity is the only true religion and that all other religions are false. There is no way to prove this. Although religions are different in their belief and practice, we cannot reasonably say that one is truer than the others. To say that Christianity is truer than other religions simply because the Bible says so is not an intelligent argument, for the same could be said of every religion that recognizes a sacred text. In fact, if truth is determined by the goodness of something, then Christianity, as it has often been practiced throughout history as a means of oppressing and subjugating others, is in a bad position to prove it is more truthful than other religions.

Misconception No. 4: Witnessing involves threatening others with the judgment of God. The classic statement in this regard is, "If you die today without being saved, you will spend eternity in hell." First of all, we are not God and we do not determine who and how God judges. Second, scaring people out of hell and into heaven is not very biblical, and it is not faithful to Jesus' call for us to share the good news. Besides, escaping a place called hell in order to get into a place called heaven is not what it means to follow Jesus. Jesus said very little, if anything, about heaven or hell.

There are probably other misconceptions I could list here, but these four should be enough to convince us that these methods are neither faithful to the gospel nor effective in calling people to follow Jesus' way of living. But if these are not the ways of being Jesus' witnesses, then what does it mean to be his witnesses? While we may shrink away from the practices and methods that those like Cameron and Comfort use, we cannot ignore Jesus' clear and straightforward command to be his witnesses.

There are numerous passages from the New Testament that we could investigate to gather an understanding of what it means to bear authentic witness to Jesus. Of course, several of these would come from the Gospels, and most notably Jesus' Great Commission in Matthew 28:19-20, where he commands his followers to go and make disciples of all peoples. But Acts 1:8 seems to me to offer a succinct and yet very rich definition of what it means to be a witness for Christ.

In Acts 1:8, Jesus tells his followers, "You will be my witnesses." As I read these words, I hear Jesus speaking more about a state of being than anything else. In other words, while action is involved in being witnesses for Christ, in that we are called to speak and do, being a witness is really more a state of existence than an action. Being a witness for Christ is an identity; an identity that is as much a part of us as our physical existence. It is who we are that leads to what we do. Thus, being a witness to Christ is not primarily an action; it is a vocation. The English word "vocation" comes from the Latin which means "calling," and it describes not so much what we do, but who we are. Vocation does not describe our employment. Rather vocation is our purpose and our way of life. Being witnesses of Christ is a way of life and a sense of being, and not simply an action through which we seek to convert others to our religious way of thinking.

But there is one very crucial point to make about our identity as witnesses. In his statement to the disciples in Acts 1:8, Jesus plainly says, "You will be my witnesses." We must always remember that we are Christ's witnesses; we bear witness to Jesus' way of living and the teachings he offered as a guide to our living. In other words, followers of Christ are not witnesses of theological doctrine or of religious practices. They are not witnesses of certain moral and political agendas. They are witnesses of the person of Jesus with whom they have an intimate relationship.

And their intimacy with Jesus, which continues after his departure through the empowerment of the Spirit, flows over into their being witnesses of him. It is not through their utilization of methods and tactics that they become witnesses. It is not through their ability to force guilt onto others that they are witnesses. It is through their relationship with the crucified and risen Christ and their empowerment by Christ's Spirit that they become witnesses of him.

There is a little comment in Acts 4 that demonstrates this very idea. As Peter preaches to those who have arrested him and John, the author of Acts tells us that those who heard Peter "recognized them as having been with Jesus." Peter and John were not off doing their own thing. They weren't creating their own movement. Rather, they were being faithful to their vocation and to their relationship to Jesus, and they were recognized as having been with Jesus.

One of the sad notes about Christianity is its long association with injustice, oppression, violence, and war. From the time of Medieval Europe, when the church carried out violence against so called heretics, to the time when slavery and segregation in this country was supported by white Christians, to more recent days when many Christians express hate towards gays and lesbians and the majority of evangelicals support torture, Christianity has often failed to be an authentic witness to the authentic Jesus.

If we are to be recognized as having been with Jesus, if we are to be authentic witnesses of Christ, then our lives and our messages must express to the world the transformative message of Jesus. But if our lives and beliefs express neglect, injustice, intolerance, exclusion, hate, violence, and war, or the support of any of these, then we are false witnesses to a false Christ. When we believe that we must stand for intolerance, hatred, violence, and oppression in order to be true to what we think God desires, we are indeed more witnesses of a false Christ than the authentic Jesus.

What is shocking to me is that many evangelicals who practice witnessing as a confrontational approach to convincing people of their guilt and sin and their need to convert people to Christianity, are often the most intolerant of people, whose intolerance and hate speech do not fit with having been with Jesus. In their form of bearing witness, they have so changed the person of Jesus that they bear false witness to who Jesus really is. Perhaps the real Jesus is too offensive to their liking, so they change Jesus to fit their own theological and political ideas. But, if the church is to be the authentic witness to the authentic Jesus, then we must become recognizable to the world as having been with the real Jesus, as having been transformed by his words, and perhaps most importantly, through practicing his radical way of living.

Coexisting, Not Competing in a Pluralistic World

Much of the problem with those folks who want to "reclaim America as a Christian nation," as they like to say, has as much or more to do with the pluralist society in which we live as it does with their perceptions that America has slipped into moral decay, which they define more often than not in very limited ways. Many of these leaders, both religious and political, feel threatened by people of other faiths, particularly those who are Muslim. Indeed, after the attacks of September 11, 2001, many reports surfaced that detailed attacks carried out against Muslim-Americans, and a few of those attacks were in fact committed against persons who the attackers believed looked like Muslims but who were not. Moreover, the 2008 presidential election campaign, and the Religious Right's attempt to derail Barack Obama's campaign, brought about a plethora of email distributions and Internet postings suggesting that Barack Obama was indeed a Muslim. In response to what is perceived as the "Islamization" of America, some states have instituted legislation that prevents the practice of *Sharia* Law and communities have stood against the construction of mosques. This is evidence that diversity, particularly religious diversity, is considered a threat by those who think America is a Christian nation.

There is no doubt that 21st century America is more pluralistic and religiously diverse than any previous century. Our knowledge of other religions has grown and our personal interactions with folks from other faiths have increased. Because of education, the media, and personal encounters with people of other faiths, we, more than any other generation of Americans, are conscious of other religions, although we are often misinformed about them, which contributes to our seeing them as either a threat to our way of life or as a misguided people in need of salvation.

The view that Christianity is the only true religion has prevailed in the West since the fourth century when the Medieval Roman Catholic Church rose to religious dominance over Europe and claimed that there was no salvation outside the church. This view continued in the Protestant traditions that originated during and after the Reformation, and it still exists in many churches today.

To be sure, not all religions are the same. There are significant differences about how we understand God, how we understand humanity, and how humans respond to God. These differences do not need to be pushed aside. But at the heart of the major world religions is a yearning to relate to something beyond the material world, beyond our human existence. The human desire to know God is also a desire to know ourselves, and to know how we are to live as humans are intended. Likewise, at the heart of these religions is the desire to create a more compassionate and just world that battles against the powers of evil and oppression. Certainly evil exists in all religions, but as we cannot prove that one religion is more evil than the others, so we cannot prove that one religion is morally superior or truer than the others.

In applying this idea to our Christian faith, we must recognize that to be a follower of Jesus is not a position of certitude from which we claim to have the eternal truth. Rather, it is a life of discipleship through which we live out the eternal quest of seeking the truth. Being Christian is not about forcing others to view Jesus as the only way to experience God. Being Christian is about being in a relationship with God and living as a person of love, goodness, and justice; virtues which other religions also seek. Indeed, we can be faithful to our Christian faith, along with its traditions, and not only coexist with people from other faiths, but more importantly, work hand in hand with all people who seek for the common good of all humanity. Doing so seems to me to be the more authentic way of being a follower of Jesus; one who seeks to emulate his humanity.

If the above is true, then why am I a Christian? I can only answer from my perspective, but perhaps some of you will share these ideas with me. First, I am a Christian because for me Jesus presents an authentic way of being human. As I wrote in the chapter on Jesus, the Gospels present Jesus as the Human One, the one who models for us the way of God. His life was devoted to liberating those who were oppressed, to challenging the political and religious powers that oppressed people, and to seeking God through the practice of the spiritual disciplines of worship, prayer, and reflection. For me, Jesus' teachings resonate with my mind and soul as that which is true, without my feeling the need to argue that another person's experience and understanding of God and religious truth is false.

Second, I am Christian because it offers to me a community of faith in which I find meaning and direction. Humans are social beings who seek community, and those who search for meaning in God are also seeking meaning in human relationships. Indeed, while we can experience God as individuals, we more truly find God in the relationships we build with other human beings. Whether I decide to be Catholic, Baptist, Presbyterian, or any other brand of Christian, I am making a choice to be a member of a community where my faith can be nurtured in loving relationships that challenge me to live out my faith. This is not to say that the choice of a faith community is made haphazardly, as if I am at the local fast food joint choosing which value meal I want. No, choosing a faith community is like finding a spouse with whom you connect on various levels, some not even measurable. It is a sense of peace that you feel when you know you want to commit the rest of your life to this person. Could I find these things in other religions? I am sure that I would. But instead of shopping around for another way to know God, I prefer to explore more deeply how I can know God through my own practice of following Jesus, even if I horribly fall short.

The Praxes of Discipleship, Not the Propositions of Theology

The Greek title given to the book of the New Testament we call "Acts" is translated into English as the "*praxes* of the apostles." This title, which probably was given to the book in the 2nd century C.E., signified the deeds of those followers of Jesus who were bearing witness to him. In classical Greek, the term *praxis*, the singular form of *praxes*, meant the practical application of a theory. In applying this idea to how the church lives faithfully in the world, we might suggest that our actions speak louder than our words. While we can spout off our theological beliefs, what we do in the name of Jesus is the real witness we bear about him. Thus, the *praxes* we carry out in the world must align with his way of living.

Yet, the church often seems to focus more on the propositions of the faith than these *praxes*, forcing folks to adhere to certain, and often very rigid, theological ideas. Theology has replaced *praxes* as the expression of faithfulness to Jesus. But this is not the message Jesus preached. I am certainly not anti-theology, for I have given most of my life to grappling with the theology that comes from the scriptures and that has been formulated throughout the history of the church. But theological propositions should not be set in stone, and theology must be an ongoing conversation that takes place in contexts and that is always fluid and malleable. In this way, theology and theological propositions remain secondary to Christian *praxes* and discipleship. Indeed, theology should only be that which serves to lead us to being more faithful in the *praxes* of discipleship. What are the key *praxes* of the church?

Praxis of Love

In reading the Hebrew and Christian scriptures, we cannot help but draw one fundamental conclusion about the essence of God; God is love. From Genesis to Revelation, the pages of the Bible sing forth that God is love. If this is true, then we must conclude that the primary characteristic of God's people must also love. While we speak about God's kingdom coming in power, it is in the power of love that God's kingdom transforms the world.

This begs the question as to what we mean by God's love. We know that God loves the world, the entirety of humanity, but what does this love mean? To answer this question we need only look once again at the person of Jesus. Christians, as I have stated before, believe that Jesus is the manifestation of God, and thus Jesus is an expression of God's perfect love for the world. Over and over the New Testament tells us that God's love is conveyed to us by the coming of Jesus. Yet, we might understand this expression of God's love in Jesus in two related ways.

In one sense, Jesus' coming to the world is the demonstration of God's love for the world. The incarnation event is the act that expresses God's love. Yet, another implication of God's love revealed in Jesus is the example Jesus gives to show how humans ought to emulate God's love. If Jesus is our example, then how we live should reflect how he lived, and particularly how he demonstrated the love of God in the world.

But what did it mean for Jesus to express God's love to the world? More important for us, what does God's love mean for how we love others, friends and foes? While these questions may have multiple answers, we can see crucial aspects of Jesus' manifestation of God's love that define what it means for followers of Jesus to share the love of God in the world.

Jesus expressed God's love in action. God does not simply feel love for the world, God has demonstrated God's love in a real event; the Christ event. We often view love as an emotion, but the person we love can only experience such love when we express it through our actions toward another. This means that love is not love until it is proven through action. But this point leads to a second significant idea about God's love.

Jesus also revealed God's love through sacrifice. Jesus defined his death as a sacrificial service to the world. Giving his life for others was the greatest of all actions one could complete. But in the context of his speaking about his own death, we find that Jesus very often defines for his followers that authentic faith and discipleship also require great sacrifice. In other words, if God has chosen to love us through a sacrificial act, giving God's own son, then we are also called to love others sacrificially.

Jesus also demonstrated God's love without limitations. No scriptural statement communicates this thought better than John 3:16: "God so loved the world." God loves all of creation, and particularly every human being on this earth. Jesus showed this love throughout his life, often choosing to love those considered unlovable in his society. In response to his model of love, we must reach beyond our own comfortableness and love not only those we consider loveable, but also those we consider unlovable, including our enemies. Yet, such love requires something most of us cannot bring ourselves to consider.

Jesus also showed God's love through his becoming vulnerable. In loving us, God chose to face life as we face life. God became not only flesh; God also became vulnerable. We do not often like to think of God as vulnerable. But God's great power is seen foremost in God's vulnerability. Indeed, without this vulnerability, God cannot truly love us, for to love another is always to become vulnerable. Our love for the world must reflect the love that God has for the world, and this certainly includes the possibility of our being vulnerable to those we love.

Praxis of Consciousness

When you read the Gospel narratives, do you ever notice how Jesus sees and hears those people ignored by others? Whether a blind beggar, a woman who has been bleeding for twelve years, or a hungry crowd, Jesus either sees them when others don't, or he sees them quite differently than others do. These encounters inform us that Jesus had an intentional consciousness of those around him.

Earlier I wrote about the consciousness of Jesus, particularly his realization of who God is and who he was in relationship to God. But Jesus also had a consciousness about humanity, and mostly of those who suffered. This awareness flowed out of his understanding of God and who he was in relationship to God. Indeed, it is what made Jesus authentically human. Such attentiveness toward those who suffered offered to his followers a model of what it meant to live under the rule of God. But what kind of consciousness did Jesus have and what patterns of living did he exhibit that offer to us a pattern for living as faithful disciples of Jesus?

Before addressing the latter question, let us answer the first by remembering that in his life, Jesus expressed the essence of God's character and love through sacrificial action and vulnerability toward humanity. Jesus' consciousness about those around him, particularly those regarded as expendable by society, was based on his understanding of God's limitless and sacrificial love. Jesus, therefore, had a clear awareness not only of his own purpose of bringing God's justice to the world, but he also had a keen consciousness of those who needed God's justice.

How should this influence our living if we choose to live according to the paradigm Jesus has set for us? First, Jesus' life and teachings should convince us that we must repent of our complacency about the injustices in our world, and that we must develop a consciousness about those who suffer. When Jesus called people to repent in response to his announcement that the kingdom of God had come, he was not calling them only to turn away from personal sins. He was calling them to repent of the sins of neglect, unconsciousness, and detachment, which are the greatest sins of humanity. As the saying goes, "The opposite of love is not hate. It is indifference." Jesus calls us to repent from lives of self-centeredness and indifference and to commit our lives to embodying God's justice in the world.

For most of us the problem is perhaps not a lack of compassion, or an unwillingness to help others, but rather a deficiency in our awareness about what really goes on in the world apart from our self-interests. Allow me to set forth the following example from common church life that clarifies my concerns. Most churches have a prayer list on which one normally finds the concerns connected to that group; someone's grandmother, uncle, friend, etc. There is nothing wrong with praying for these concerns, for they are real concerns and God cares for each one. But why don't these prayer lists also mention the larger sufferings and injustices of the world, such as hunger, war, intolerance, etc.?

We could push this further by stating that many churches do not set aside a time during worship to pray for those who suffer from injustice. Moreover, Bible studies and sermons are mostly about us, about how to live better lives, about our relationships to God as individuals, and about how to get to heaven. There is nothing wrong with this, for such teachings are part of being Christian, but these concerns are a significantly small fraction of what it means to follow Christ. In our places of worship, we should press our thinking about God and about what God is doing in the world beyond ourselves, and we must seek God's greater desire for us and for the world, which is to bring God's justice to all. We should struggle more with the suffering and oppression across our world and not so much focus on how God meets our needs.

When we do this, we will not only become aware of the greater needs of our world, we will also become mindful of how God sees those who suffer. And when our collective consciousness is raised, we can respond to God's call to seek justice for those who do not have justice. When we reach the point of abandoning ourselves, our desires, and even our very lives, we will more authentically live out the wisdom of Jesus.

Praxis of Service

In the Gospel narratives, Jesus often defines his life as one of service, and he repeatedly clarifies that those who desire to be participants is his movement must choose to live in humble service toward others. Many of Jesus' words express such teachings, but more evocative are the actions of humble service that Jesus performs. One story in particular is striking.

In John 13 we find the narrative of Jesus gathering with his disciples to eat the Passover Meal. Jesus, knowing that the time of his death was approaching, stands up from the table, takes off his outer robe, puts a towel around him, and begins to wash the feet of his disciples. While the image of Jesus doing this has become familiar to us, it must have been shocking to his disciples. The act of Jesus, their master, washing their feet was, as they saw it, a deed only to be carried out by lowly slaves when guests entered a house from the dirty road. Such a subservient act was not something the disciples expected Jesus to do.

However, the washing of the disciples' feet was not simply Jesus performing another act of service. Rather, in putting on the towel, the official uniform that branded a person as a house slave, Jesus was clarifying that he was not just executing an act of service; he was identifying himself as a servant. His performance of the lowliest of tasks was an image that defined who he believed himself to be, the suffering servant of humanity.

But what does it mean that Jesus labeled himself as a servant and, more importantly for us, what does it mean that he commanded his followers to be servants? To answer this, an interesting point needs to be made about how Jesus saw his mission of service in the context of the Roman Empire. The Romans were notorious for the domination they maintained through military power and cultural arrogance. Such attitudes permeated society as people sought to live for themselves, ruling and dominating others. There was no genuine concern for others, as most people looked out for themselves. In creating an alternative empire, however, Jesus informed his followers that this way of living was not the ethical norm of the empire of God. The ethics of God's kingdom required service, and through both his teachings and his actions, Jesus defined service as that which is sacrificial; the giving of oneself for the good of others. True greatness in the empire of God, according to Jesus, is not found in conquering and dominating; it is found in being last and in being servant of all.

Like Jesus' culture, where people wanted to rule over one another with arrogant domination, our society tells us, explicitly and implicitly, that power is what brings victory. Financial power, political power, and military power are the ambitions of our society, and the church has not only tolerated these, it has embraced them. But the gospel message is clear. Sacrificial service is the radical way of living for those who seek the kingdom of God, and those who seek to be powerful in this world are cut off from God's kingdom. Individuals and societies that seek to coerce through domination and exploitation in this world are excluded from God's kingdom, for God's kingdom is intended for those who answer the call to be lowly servants.

But to become true servants requires us to repent of our thoughts and acts of superiority and to embrace humility. We are often guilty of considering ourselves superior to others because of our race, our nationality, our wealth, our military strength, and even our religion. But such arrogance has no place in the kingdom of God. We cannot have the view that we are somehow financially, intellectually, culturally, militarily, or even religiously better than the rest of the world. Instead, followers of Jesus must see themselves as Jesus saw himself, in solidarity with humanity and not as rulers over the world. Our culture does not make us superior. Our power does not make us stronger. And our religion certainly does not make us godlier. Attitudes of superiority and attempts to dominate others will not bring God's kingdom of justice into the world. God's kingdom will come only through self-sacrificing acts of humble service that reflect Jesus' model of being a servant of humanity.

Praxis of Sharing

In Luke 12 Jesus tells a parable about a rich man who had plenty. In fact, the man had so much grain that he decided to tear down his barns and build bigger ones. This rich man believed that because of his new windfall he was set for a life of ease and pleasure. Yet, in a shocking twist of events, the man's life came to an unexpected end, and his abundance was wasted. He had assumed that his surplus of grain would keep him comfortable for years to come, but instead his life was demanded of him that night, and his excess became useless.

In reading this parable, most of us would agree that the sin of the man was greed. He horded what he could for himself so that he could live out his days in ease. But why is greed a sin? We often consider greed for wealth and possessions as a sin because it puts these things in place of God. In other words, we view greed as a transgression because when we are greedy we make wealth our god. While this is true, it is so only partly. Greed is a sin, not because it puts wealth in the place of God, but because it prevents us from sharing what we have with our neighbors. In telling this particular parable in an agrarian society where most people survived on daily rations of food, Jesus conveyed very clearly that this man's sin is against God, but only because his sin is against his neighbors who suffer in poverty while he lounges in plenty.

Jesus had a great deal to say about how we view and use our wealth and possessions. Indeed, he said more on this subject than any others, including salvation. One of his most famous statements comes from the Sermon on the Mount where he states that we cannot serve both God and money. But what is particularly arresting when we read thoroughly all of Jesus' teachings on money and possessions, is that we discover that he always spoke of giving them up in the search for God's kingdom. In fact, a careful reading of the Gospels seems to suggest that joining the Jesus movement of the first century meant that one must renounce using one's wealth for selfish indulgence and one ought to embrace the call to use one's possessions to help those in need. To state his teachings more directly, the demands of discipleship call us to seriously consider giving up our wealth and possessions as we seek to follow Jesus.

How does Jesus' demand to relinquish material assets pertain to our modern existence? While a response to such a call may not require us to take vows of poverty like St. Francis of Assisi and Mother Theresa, Jesus' command most certainly means that we must choose to live lives of simplicity. As followers of a homeless vagrant, Christians, both as individuals and as churches, should seek to reexamine our desire for material possessions in light of Jesus' commands and actions. In doing so, we can accomplish Jesus' call to express our love for both God and others by sharing our wealth with others. A choice to live modestly, a choice to dematerialize our lives, will free us to share with those in need. This choice also reflects the essence of God, who in Jesus, became poor for us.

In a world where abject poverty is pervasive, people of faith must choose to live simply and avoid hoarding money and possessions. Doing so will mean that we will have more to share with others; with neighbors, strangers, and those we call our enemies. Furthermore, this lifestyle both imitates the life of Jesus and is a means to bringing God's kingdom of justice into the world.

Praxis of Embrace

A remarkable story is situated in the book of Acts that exposes Peter's mindset toward people he considered unclean. Peter is praying on a rooftop when he falls into a deep trance. He has a vision of a great sheet coming down from heaven on which he sees all kinds of animals. A voice then commands him to eat the animals, but

Peter refuses because, for him and other Jews of the first century, the eating of these animals made one unclean before God. The voice, which we are to assume is God's, reasserts the original command by clarifying that what God has made clean, is clean.

This story, however, is not about animals, clean or unclean; it is about Peter's prejudices and his exclusion of others from full participation in the community of God. Peter understood the well-established boundaries between purity and impurity, boundaries that faithful Jews of the first century dare not cross. Such boundaries prevented one from exposure to certain things that were considered unclean. Among those who could be viewed as polluted were the diseased, the lame, sinners of all sorts, and, in Peter's case, the Gentiles.

Jesus also understood the boundaries between purity and impurity that existed in his day. In fact, one of the frequent accusations made against him was that he congregated with the wrong kind of impure people, even to the point of sharing intimate meals with them. However, regardless of whether they were sinners and tax collectors, women of questionable character, or those with unclean diseases, each societal outcast found acceptance in Jesus' community. Why? Because Jesus also understood that in him God was establishing a kingdom in which the boundaries between those who were pure and those who were deemed impure were torn down, and he made conscious choices to cross those boundaries to share intimate space and table fellowship with them.

What does it mean to exclude others? Yale theologian Miroslav Volf sees the sin of exclusion inherent in four human actions.[1] According to Volf, we exclude others when we abandon or ignore them and their needs. We also exclude others when we seek to assimilate them to be like us. We practice exclusion of others when we dominate them and force our own views and way of life on them. And worse still, we exclude others when we seek to exterminate them. In light of Volf's comprehensive description of the sin

---

[1] Miroslav Volf, *Exclusion and Embrace: A Theological Exploration of Identity, Otherness, and Reconciliation* (Nashville: Abingdon Press, 1996), esp. 72-79.

of exclusion, each one of us is in a position of guilt. How shall we remedy this situation?

When it comes to the issue of exclusion in our own culture, we hear two dominant voices pulling us to and fro. On one side we here our secular culture call us to practice tolerance. The other voice comes from religious fundamentalists who preach to us that tolerance is a sin. So where does the antidote to the sin of exclusion rest? Is it rejection of tolerance or acceptance of tolerance? Should we hide behind a false gospel that calls us to separate ourselves from those not like us, which only reinforces our stereotypes of others and increases our hatred? Or should we conform to the meaninglessness of tolerance, knowing that tolerance merely calls us to grit our teeth and bear with others not like us, yet keeps us at a distance from them? The biblical answer lies neither in the denunciation of tolerance nor the reluctant acceptance of tolerance. The answer lies in the person and practice of Jesus, who came into the world not to cast us aside, and surely not to tolerate us, but rather to embrace us.

If we accept the historical reality that Jesus lived the way the Gospels say he lived, as an intimate friend to those considered impure to his society, then those of us who claim to follow Jesus can do nothing less than to model his way of life. But if we reject his example by choosing to exclude others, then we mock God's embrace of us, and we come dangerously close to being outsiders to God's kingdom.

Where are the boundaries of exclusion we have established between ourselves and those we consider outsiders? Race, ethnicity, gender, religion, social standing, economic status, and sexual orientation are all areas of identity where in some form or fashion we practice exclusion in all its forms. But if we are to bear witness to Jesus' way of living, then we must repent of our sin of exclusion, cross the boundaries we have set between ourselves and others, and embrace all persons as God's children.

Praxis of Peace

At the beginning of his Sermon on the Mount in Matthew 5, Jesus makes nine statements that would be enough to offer us a guide to living the way God would have us live even if they were the only extant words of Jesus we had. Each statement promises blessings if we live according to what is implicitly demanded by Jesus' words. Unfortunately, his demands are not easy, as he tells us that to find true happiness we must be poor, be mournful, be meek, hunger for righteousness, be merciful, and endure persecution in the name of Jesus.

One of these sayings, however, strikes me as particularly important for our world today and for the church's call to live according to Jesus' teachings. In the seventh Beatitude Jesus says, "Blessed are the peacemakers, for they will be called children of God." Given the fact that this statement appears in the list of these important ethical values, peacemaking must assuredly be a core action for Jesus' followers. Peacemaking not only reflects Jesus' teachings, it also reflects the life of Jesus who came as the Prince of Peace. But what is required to be peacemakers and why must we be peacemakers?

The kind of peacemaking Jesus commands requires non-violent responses to evil. One of Jesus' most controversial statements also comes to us through Matthew's Sermon on the Mount. Jesus states, "When someone strikes you on one cheek, turn and offer to him the other one." While many have tried to live true to this instruction of Jesus, more often than not Christians have found his command to turn from violence unsettling. But we cannot negotiate with Jesus at this point, for his statement is very straightforward. If this is true, then why do we tend to avoid Jesus' clear command to turn the other cheek as an essential part of being peacemakers?

The answer to that question lies in our failure to see that Jesus' definition of peacemaking also requires forgiveness. The central message of Scripture is that God so loved the world, and in God's love, God has forgiven the world. But God's forgiveness is not based on our paying restitution or in our suffering a penalty. God's forgiveness flows from God's unconditional love for humanity and a desire to make peace with us.

Our biggest problem in practicing this kind of forgiveness, and therefore our greatest hindrance to making peace, is that we are vengeful. Our culture tells us that revenge is a necessary part of justice, and when we as individuals, or as a group, or as a nation are wronged, it is only right, even expected, that we seek revenge against the wrongdoers. While the message of the world is that vengeance is right, and making people pay for the harm they cause us is good, the message of Jesus calls us to something greater that reflects God's own character and action—forgiveness. Forgiveness is the necessary action that leads to peacemaking.

While Jesus' teachings on peacemaking apply to those of us who seek to reconcile with those who have hurt us, peacemaking also extends to conflicts among groups of people, whether local conflicts or wars on the global front. The waging of any war brings destruction to the lives of ordinary people, and will not establish lasting peace. The Christian community should condemn such hostilities, because Jesus never called his followers to take up the weapons of warfare and kill their enemies. He has called us to take up the cross of self-sacrifice through which we can find love for our enemies.

Two statements by Dr. Martin Luther King seem relevant to this topic. Dr. King stated, "Wars are poor chisels for carving out peaceful tomorrows." Jesus also understood that war could never assure the world of peace; only peacemaking brings lasting peace. Dr. King also said, "Peace is not the absence of war, but the presence of justice." God's coming kingdom can bring lasting peace into the world, but only when we practice making peach through seeking justice for our neighbors and our enemies.

Following the Crucified Jesus

One of the dominant themes in the Gospel of Mark is the journey that Jesus and his disciples travel. Often, this wandering band is pictured on the road moving toward, as we discover through reading the story, Jerusalem, the holy city of David. As the narrative of Mark moves forward, however, Jerusalem begins to come into clear view, and Jesus begins to point this out to them.

Most likely those who followed Jesus knew they were headed to Jerusalem; what faithful Jew would not know the direction to

Jerusalem? So Jesus' acknowledgement that they are headed to Jerusalem seems out of place, unless the mention of the direction in which they are headed is intended to mean something. Why does Jesus state specifically that they are headed for Jerusalem? For what purpose did the disciples think they were headed for Jerusalem? Did their understanding of trip to Jerusalem match that of Jesus?

Perhaps they thought that when they reached Jerusalem, Jesus would take his rightful place as King of Israel and overthrow the Romans. Perhaps they followed Jesus, hoping that they would be participants in this rule of Jesus in David's city. Most likely they believed that Jesus' purpose in continuing on the road to Jerusalem was so that he would be made king and, consequently, they would share in that kingly power.

This expectation is seen most clearly in the request two of Jesus' disciples make as their band moves even closer to Jerusalem. The brothers, James and John, come to Jesus with the bold request, "Grant us to sit, one at your right and one at your left, in your glory" (Mark 10:37). These disciples seem to understand that following Jesus leads to glory, but they fail to understand that there is no glory apart from the cross that looms in Jerusalem. In Mark's story, Jesus had spoken to them two other times before this exchange about what would happen in Jerusalem; he would be arrested, beaten and killed. But somehow they failed to hear, or perhaps, refused to hear his words. Instead they continued to see the movement toward Jerusalem as a move toward power and glory and not one that would lead to suffering and death.

The specifics of the request made by the brothers should not be missed. James and John were seeking seats of authority by requesting places on the right and left of Jesus. Jesus affirms that there are such seats, but that they are reserved for whom they have been prepared by God. But the only other place in Mark where people are said to be on the right and left of Jesus is in the crucifixion scene of 15:32-52, where someone is crucified on his right and someone else is crucified on his left. Moreover, just before we read of these two other crucified victims on either side of Jesus, we are told of the inscription that read, "King of the Jews."

What all of this says to us is that the kingly glory of Jesus in Mark's narrative is found in his death on the cross, and those who are at the right and left of Jesus in glory are those who take their places on the right and left of Jesus in crucifixion. For Jesus, glory comes not in the heavens, but in the cross.

This overturns our own ideas of greatness and power. Greatness does not come in worldly thrones, but in the throne of a cross. Power does not come by ruling over people, but by serving others. In opposition to the disciples, Jesus was living out true greatness and power by going down the road to Jerusalem that led to the cross.

When I was getting ready to preach one Sunday morning, I sat on one of the front pews in the church. At the end of the pew there was a stack of music books. As we stood to sing, I happened to glance at the title of the books, which read, "Easy Gospel Arrangements." We often are like James and John in that we want easy gospel arrangements. Certainly the gospel is freely offered to all, but it is not cheap in its demands. The real gospel of the real Jesus calls us to give up ourselves in self-sacrificial service to God and others by taking up the cross and following Jesus. Only in doing this can we reclaim the church's place and mission.

Questions for Reflection and Discussion

1. Read the quote from Gandhi at the beginning of this chapter. What did Gandhi mean and why is his statement so troubling?

2. How has the institutional church distanced itself from the authentic teachings of Jesus? How has your congregation distanced itself from the authentic teachings of Jesus?

3. How might the church reclaim its identity as the broken body of Christ?

4. Why is it important for the church to remain a prophetic voice to culture and politics?

5. What is the relationship between Christianity and other world religions? How have we demonized these other religions? In what ways can we work with people of other faith to accomplish the common good and still keep our Christian identity?

6. How would our witness for Christ change if we focused less on theological propositions and more on the praxes of discipleship?

7. In what ways can your church carry out these praxes?

ALSO FROM ENERGION PUBLICATIONS

Perhaps those of us who are in different streams of Christian thought need to consider that others also have something to contribute, that their disagreements with us do not represent apostasy or heresy but rather their unique and valuable experience of God.

When Weiss walks you through the Gospel of John, the maze turns to amazement. You will discover another world with all the favorable conditions for a better life.

Abraham Terian
St. Nersess Armenian Seminary

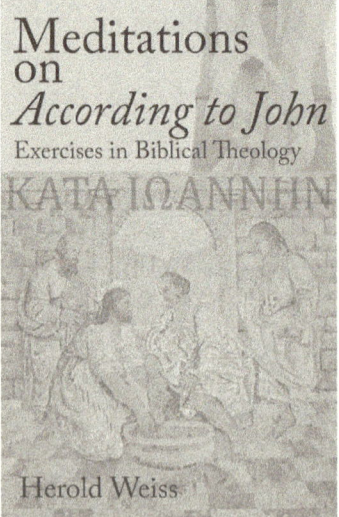

More from Energion Publications

Personal Study
Holy Smoke! Unholy Fire	Bob McKibben	$14.99
The Jesus Paradigm	David Alan Black	$17.99
When People Speak for God	Henry Neufeld	$17.99
The Sacred Journey	Chris Surber	$11.99

Christian Living
It's All Greek to Me	David Alan Black	$3.99
Grief: Finding the Candle of Light	Jody Neufeld	$8.99
My Life Story	Becky Lynn Black	$14.99
Crossing the Street	Robert LaRochelle	$16.99
Life as Pilgrimage	David Moffett-Moore	14.99

Bible Study
Learning and Living Scripture	Lentz/Neufeld	$12.99
From Inspiration to Understanding	Edward W. H. Vick	$24.99
Philippians: A Participatory Study Guide	Bruce Epperly	$9.99
Ephesians: A Participatory Study Guide	Robert D. Cornwall	$9.99
Ecclesiastes: A Participatory Study Guide	Russell Meek	$9.99

Theology
Creation in Scripture	Herold Weiss	$12.99
Creation: the Christian Doctrine	Edward W. H. Vick	$12.99
The Politics of Witness	Allan R. Bevere	$9.99
Ultimate Allegiance	Robert D. Cornwall	$9.99
History and Christian Faith	Edward W. H. Vick	$9.99
The Journey to the Undiscovered Country	William Powell Tuck	$9.99
Process Theology	Bruce G. Epperly	$4.99

Ministry
Clergy Table Talk	Kent Ira Groff	$9.99
Out of This World	Darren McClellan	$24.99

Generous Quantity Discounts Available
Dealer Inquiries Welcome
Energion Publications — P.O. Box 841
Gonzalez, FL 32560
Website: http://energionpubs.com
Phone: (850) 525-3916

www.ingramcontent.com/pod-product-compliance
Lightning Source LLC
LaVergne TN
LVHW011209080426
835508LV00007B/688